SELF-LOVE
LOVING YOUR SOUL
Twenty-Two Stories of Self-Love

ALICIA ANN WADE

BALBOA.PRESS
A DIVISION OF HAY HOUSE

Copyright © 2023 Alicia Ann Wade.

All rights reserved. No part of this book may be used or reproduced by any means, graphic, electronic, or mechanical, including photocopying, recording, taping or by any information storage retrieval system without the written permission of the author except in the case of brief quotations embodied in critical articles and reviews.

Balboa Press books may be ordered through booksellers or by contacting:

Balboa Press
A Division of Hay House
1663 Liberty Drive
Bloomington, IN 47403
www.balboapress.com.au
AU TFN: 1 800 844 925 (Toll Free inside Australia)
AU Local: (02) 8310 7086 (+61 2 8310 7086 from outside Australia)

Because of the dynamic nature of the Internet, any web addresses or links contained in this book may have changed since publication and may no longer be valid. The views expressed in this work are solely those of the author and do not necessarily reflect the views of the publisher, and the publisher hereby disclaims any responsibility for them.

The author of this book does not dispense medical advice or prescribe the use of any technique as a form of treatment for physical, emotional, or medical problems without the advice of a physician, either directly or indirectly. The intent of the author is only to offer information of a general nature to help you in your quest for emotional and spiritual well-being. In the event you use any of the information in this book for yourself, which is your constitutional right, the author and the publisher assume no responsibility for your actions.

Any people depicted in stock imagery provided by Getty Images are models, and such images are being used for illustrative purposes only. Certain stock imagery © Getty Images.

Print information available on the last page.

ISBN: 978-1-9822-9754-1 (sc)
ISBN: 978-1-9822-9755-8 (e)

Balboa Press rev. date: 07/03/2023

SELF-LOVE
LOVING YOUR SOUL

Twenty-Two Stories of Self-Love

Alexandra De La Cruz
Ali Moustafa
Alpa Sancheti
Brent Lindsay
Christine Innes
Deleine Gavin-Cox
Hazel Vertley
Josh Solomon
Kate Taylor
Katherine Jackat
Kathryn Dawe
Kelly Kingston
Laila Ansari
Lisa Infante
Natalie Rubria
Nicole Pirrie
Rhonda Dodds
Shanki Jayawickrama
Shaima Al Abbasi
Tanya Leach
Tasha Dziesinski
Titin Mubarokah
Ursh Arthars (Foreword)

Endorsements

"This chapter is a reminder that while circumstances can shape us, they do not define us.

'Self care is not Selfish' demonstrates how learning to love ourselves, and care for ourselves, is a journey that takes time but also great strength. Kathyrn's story is not one to shy away from the harsh lessons learnt but more importantly than that - it is a beacon that there is hope for change, growth and a different life for anyone out there who might be stuck in the story of their upbringing."

Love & Magic,

Nikki Wouters
Intuitive Life & Business Coach

"This chapter helps by giving you tools and ideas to decipher self love in your life. I hope that you get what you need out of reading this as I did and it helps you to be a better you for you. I agree that self love changes in different seasons we go through in our lives. I enjoyed breaking down the years as suggested and reflecting on where I was personally at that time. In this fast paced world where everything is at our fingertips, it is truly important to self reflect and find what self love means to us individually. Are we people pleasers? Are we thriving, surviving, drowning? Only you can know."

Anna Dunek

"Self-love means having a high regard for your well-being and happiness, and Self-love means taking care of your needs and not sacrificing your well-being to please others." Sounds simple, right? I'm a mom of seven and a Registered Nurse, two callings that revolve around caring for and serving other people. I'm surrounded by people, especially women, who are in the same sphere. It can be so easy to give all our energy away as we serve those around us. By walking through the fire, I've learned that I do not have the ability to care for others properly if I do not first prioritize myself. Unfortunately, it's sometimes easier said than done. I love the emphasis Rhonda puts on being intentional about our own self-love and self-care. Life gets so busy and just as I need to protect my time with the people I love (my husband, children, friends), I need to be intentional about doing things that are going to feed my soul and keep me feeling energized, or at least able to tackle another day. For me, that often consists of going to the gym, hiking, bike riding, or just being out in the sun. As pointed out in the definition of self-love, this is a desirable, rather than narcissistic trait! It's good, not selfish. What an affirming reminder.

M.J.Volkers

"Overall, Shanki's piece has a lot of heart and clarity. Very comprehensively written too.
    Well done! a journey well worth the arduor!"

Anon

"Tasha is a deep, thoughtful and moving writer, which beautifully and perfectly emulates the deep, thoughtful and moving woman that she is. Tasha's courage and authenticity is contagious, and there are few humans that I've known who have been as open with their hearts through their own pain as they are available for others in the midst of theirs. Tasha's words on, and experience with, grief will comfort you and make you feel less alone in your pain as she shares how she's been moving through hers."

Julia Kristina, MA Psych

"Tasha's writing style connects with the reader on a personal & emotional level. She writes from the Whole Heart & shares her experiences in a refreshingly transparent & authentic way. Tasha has the ability to go deep into detail while also providing perspective over the story. Her profound resolve & commitment to an ever-increasing level of self-forgiveness & self-compassion will resonate with many like-minded readers; serving as an inspiration to continue on their own journeys."

Tess René Schultz
Master Therapeutic + Transformational Coach | Author | Speaker

"Tasha's writing should inspire each of us to know there is life beyond grief. Through her pain, she has become a beautiful butterfly! She is a strong woman whom I admire."

Nancy Frazier

"Tasha's experience of grief is relatable and the way she expresses herself made me feel that my experiences with grief are validated. I have lost many relatives and I also had a friend who became estranged with me. I felt hope reading her chapter because as she expressed her pain and sadness, she also expressed her healing and that gives me hope that I can heal from grief too."

Chris Hill

"Shaima's chapter is a heartfelt and honest exploration of your personal journey towards self-love. You effectively convey your challenges and transformations you experienced, which provide insights to me as the reader and will do so for many other readers. The chapter captures the essence of self-love as an ongoing journey rather than a destination, emphasizing the choices and commitments you made to honour and cherish yourself.

You openly share your struggles, from the emptiness you felt as a stay-at-home mother to the impact of your cousin's death to cancer as well as the weight you carried yearning for external validation. These personal experiences add authenticity to your narrative and makes it easy for the reader to connect with your story as they reflect on their own lives.

The chapter also highlights the importance of self-reflection which leads to the realisation that self-love goes beyond surface-level activities. You discuss the impact of childhood experiences, such as your parents' divorce, and how it shaped your beliefs about yourself. By acknowledging and challenging your beliefs, you demonstrate the power of being self-aware as you journey towards self-love.

Your motivation and commitment in pursuing your dreams

while navigating motherhood and professional development are inspiring. The way you describe the embracing of the chaos in your life and finding opportunities for growth in unexpected situations resonates with me and with all readers who may be facing their own obstacles. Your commitment displayed to personal growth and the joy you derive from it, serves as a testament to how self-love can transform anyone.

The inclusion of your religious practices, such as prayer, gratitude, and self-care, adds a beautiful layer to your chapter. It highlights the importance of incorporating one's personal values and beliefs into your self-love journey. This can demonstrate to others the individual nature of self-love and will encourage readers to explore their own beliefs and practices which can contribute to their well-being.

Overall, your chapter effectively conveys the importance of self-care on many levels that ultimately leads to self-love and growth."

Hadieya Ahmed

"I really enjoyed reading Alpa's The Tree that learnt to blossom.

I have had the pleasure of knowing Alpa for a few years and her writing reads like she's sitting opposite you, having a chat over a cuppa.

I particularly resonated with the reference to the inner critic haunting me, leaving me with self-doubt and uncertainty. This self-doubt crippled me for years in terms of my self-belief in my work and my ability to lead a team. And her insightful reference to 'going down a spiral of shame and self-doubt" was like she was reading my mind when all this happened. I only wish I had had Alpa in my life at that difficult time. And I am sure that anyone reading this who is going through a similar tough time will take solace and comfort from reading this beautiful tale and knowing they are not alone.

Congratulations, Alpa, for your insights, your wise counsel and your compassion. A true friend. A fabulous coach. And a wonderful woman."

Justine Rosen

"In a powerful chapter, Alpa takes us on an emotional journey of self-discovery and personal growth. Faced with a crumbling marriage and a life that no longer aligned with her true self, she finds herself standing at a crossroads, torn between the safety of familiarity and the unknown. The rawness of her emotions is palpable as she reflects on the pain, self-doubt, and confusion that consumed her. Through introspection and the support of loved ones, she embarks on a path of healing and self-acceptance. I love that Alpa's writing style is both vulnerable and empowering, allowing you to connect with her pain and empowerment. Her exploration of self-compassion and self-love resonates deeply, reminding us of the importance of nurturing a healthy relationship with ourselves. This chapter serves as a reminder that even in our darkest moments, we have the strength to choose a path that leads us to our true selves."

Matt Lavars

"I have known Deleine for many years now, at times when we lost touch, the universe seemed to just keep bringing us back together.

We were clearly destined to be in each other's lives, "your vibe attracts your tribe"!

Having been on my own journey of feeling unworthy and finding self-love, I was moved by reading Deleine's story and could relate to many of the feelings she described.

The power of gratitude and self-love really comes through and I couldn't help but smile at times to see the positive impacts they have had on her life.

Deleine is someone who inspires me all the time with what she has overcome and what she has achieved."

Michaela White

"Reading through Dels Self Love Chapter has resonated with me to the point it has taken me back to my own teen years. While I didn't suffer the loss of a parent, I experienced resentment and what I thought at the time was hatred from one of mine. Bullying, people pleasing, self-destructive behaviour and feeling like an outsider… I went through all of these things and have learned how my experience contributed to my own lack of self-worth and desperate need to please everyone at the expense of my own identity. If only we'd known we weren't the only ones!

"I just wanted anyone in my life to love me" is a quote that stands out because so much of growing up we are taught that being loved by others is the ultimate goal, nobody ever teaches you that it starts with you. I am grateful to Del for sharing her story and highlighting how important it is to accept who we are and the steps we can take to reach that point ourselves.

My favourite quote from this story is "I love myself enough to put myself first and not feel guilty" because I believe that is one of the ultimate goals. I loved reading Del's journey and how she has worked to achieve just that."

Vanessa Ornsby

"The chapter on self-love in this book that Kathryn wrote, was truly inspiring. It helped me to see things in a whole new light and allowed me to embrace and appreciate myself on a deeper level. The messages and lessons provided were both practical and insightful, and gave me the tools I needed to pursue a true sense of love and acceptance for who I am. I would highly recommend this book to anyone who is struggling to believe in themselves and know their worth, as it truly has the power to transform the way you think about yourself and your relationship with others. This chapter alone has made such a positive impact on my life, and I'm excited to put what I've learned into practice and continue on my journey towards self-love and acceptance."

Angelique Ferris

"I have so much love and appreciation for this chapter. Self-love is a long and sometimes gruelling journey and this writer really captures this process. It is difficult when the people who should have been the most present in our life are the most distant. It can have a rippling effect and make us feel like we're not worthy of anyone's love. Hazel notes that although she still holds some pain from the past the love for her daughter is so healing. What an uplifting story about becoming the adult and parent you wish you had yourself as a child.

It is so true what Hazel writes about self-love being an ongoing process. Old habits and bad self-talk are hard to break and I found Hazel's tips for improving self- love very helpful."

Jessica Berry
Stay at home mum

"Incredibly powerful, moving, and thought-provoking. Lisa's raw, honest depiction of trauma, and the lack of self-love and forgiveness in life opens the mind to reflection. As someone who has battled with self-love and forgiveness after experiencing what Lisa defines as acute, chronic, and complex trauma—the trauma trifecta—in childhood and adolescence, Lisa's words gave me greater clarity about who I was, where I'm now at in life and how I've begun forgiven and begun practicing self-love as I've progressed from my 40s into my 50s."

Tricia Leanne Snell
The Body Better Coach & Author of The Body Better Blueprint.

"As someone who has struggled with self-esteem and self-worth, this chapter has been a beacon of light and a lifeline in my journey towards self-acceptance. Lisa's wise words resonated deeply with my own childhood experiences, born first-generation to Italian migrants with similar conflicting expectations placed on me, especially as the first born and a role model for my other siblings. No wonder I have placed so much pressure on myself my whole life!

Lisa's guidance and insights will allow you to cultivate a newfound sense of love and compassion for yourself. Through powerful exercises and thought-provoking prompts, I was able to explore my inner thoughts and beliefs, confronting self-limiting beliefs and replacing them with empowering affirmations.

Lisa has not only helped me to embrace my imperfections but has also taught me the importance of self-care and setting healthy boundaries. It has instilled in me the understanding that self-love is not selfish, but rather an essential foundation for personal growth and wellbeing; to silence my inner critic, embrace my uniqueness, and foster a genuine love and appreciation for who I am.

This self-love chapter will become your trusted companion on the journey to self-discovery, and I highly recommend it to anyone seeking to embark on their own path of self-love and self-acceptance."

Mary Galouzis
FOUNDER / CEO, TALK OUT LOUD AUSTRALIA

"Through personal anecdotes and insightful reflections, Lisa explains the importance of self-love and how it is often lacking in our lives. She provides a clear distinction between self-love and dimming our light for the sake of others' expectations or opinions. Lisa skilfully highlights the traits and behaviours that demonstrate self-love versus those that diminish it.

What I found truly inspiring about this chapter is that it doesn't paint self-love as a destination to be reached but rather an ongoing process of self-discovery, growth, and self-care. Lisa emphasises that self-love is like a muscle that needs to be flexed regularly, and she provides practical examples and techniques to nurture this essential aspect of our well-being.

Reading this chapter reminded me of the importance of self-love and the impact it can have on all aspects of our lives. I highly recommend this book chapter to anyone who wants to embark on a journey of self-discovery, self-acceptance, and self-love. Through self-love, we can heal, grow, and create a life filled with positivity, joy, and resilience. Lisa's authentic storytelling and practical insights make it an engaging and transformative read. Prepare to be inspired and empowered as you delve into the world of self-love and unlock its transformative power in your own life."

Alice Schaefer
Owner & Founder, EMPOWERED by Alice

"As children we are taught to be kind and generous and thoughtful of others - and to ALWAYS be nice; but rarely are we taught to do this for ourselves and to put ourselves first. Society seems to promote 'martyrdom' and that when you are flat out and back to back busy - that THIS is the sign of success. Never has this been further from the truth!

Self-love is hard - and often perceived as conceited.

Lisa's book was a revelation in self-love and care. If we don't love ourselves, how can we possibly show others how to love us? Sadly 'people pleaser' and 'doormat' were a part of my regular vocabulary TO MYSELF. What the hell was I doing?!!

My self-love cup wasn't empty - rather the complete opposite - it was full of everyone else's sludge! Undrinkable putrid sludge. I was choking trying to drink what others had left behind - wasn't good enough for them - but for some reason I thought it was good enough for me!

You are worth this book. This life changing book - full of positive affirmations of self-love. You are worth it! Life is short - so just DO IT!"

Michelle Jewels-Parsons
Celebrant, Author and End of Life Companion

"After reading Lisa's chapter on self-love, so much of what she wrote resonated with me. I have done a lot of work for myself in this space. I love how relatable this text is for many people, and how Lisa shares so much of her own journey to self-love. It creates so much awareness about the messaging we receive as we grow up and how we can change it without feeling the need to please those we love.

I particularly like the part where Lisa shares that although she was told that what she said mattered and she could be anything she wanted to be, it was also conditional. I enjoyed the tips for creating more self-love in life, particularly blocking out time and attention for ourselves to fill up our own cup, by connecting back to what we love and what brings us joy. This is so important, and is the most unselfish thing we can do, not only for ourselves but for those around us.

I loved Lisa's section on forgiveness, for both self and others. This is such an important part of understanding ourselves, letting go of the old, and making space for the new and all that we desire.

This is a great read for both those new to self-love and those who are well rehearsed in it. Definitely give it a read if you are wanting to learn more, or simply just need a reminder about the importance of self-love and how to create it."

Sarah Molloy
Holistic Health & Healing

"Lisa's chapter on self-love practices left me really moved. Like, tears flowing kind of moved! As someone who tries to practice self-love already, the meditation on forgiveness unexpectedly touched something deep in me, uncovering an obvious need I have for forgiveness for myself that I now need to continue working on.

Lisa's beautifully written story and passionate words really resonated with me, having grown up in an environment that didn't celebrate emotional expression and really prioritised putting others before yourself. The analogies she used to emphasise the importance of self-love were really clarifying, and the practices I learnt are ones that I've just written down in my journal for daily practice.

What a heartfelt reminder of the transformative power of self-care and acceptance, I'm so grateful Lisa! I highly recommend anyone seeking a touching and introspective look at themselves to give this a read."

Terri Williams
Founder & Creative Director, Studio Sondar

CONTENTS

Foreword xxiii
Mirror Mirror On The Wall:
A letter from the Editor xxix

Chapter 1   What is the Ratio you spend on Life's
             obligations compared to time spent on self-love? 1
Chapter 2   An Idle Tuesday Afternoon 13
Chapter 3   That Inner Voice 24
Chapter 4   Self-care is not Selfish 35
Chapter 5   The 9R Process Mindset 44
Chapter 6   The Hero Within & The Hero Without 52
Chapter 7   THE YES-A-HOLIC - Questioning everything 68
Chapter 8   Your Pathway to Self-Love 86
Chapter 9   Titin I Forgot 100
Chapter 10   The Tree That Learned To Blossom 115
Chapter 11   Grief, the highest form of Self-Love 128
Chapter 12   How I was Catapulted into the Journey of
             Self-Love 141
Chapter 13   From Fear to Love to Living My Dreams! 151
Chapter 14   What is Self-Love, To Put It Down To A
             Single Sentence? 169

Chapter 15	The Goddess Within 179
Chapter 16	Embrace Self Love 199
Chapter 17	Self-Compassion is Self-Love 208
Chapter 18	Self-love is a Lifelong Journey That Demands Patience, Commitment, and Ongoing Self-Care ... 220
Chapter 19	The Pseudo Russian Princess................................ 228
Chapter 20	Learning How To Live, Lead, And Love With Self-Love 243
Chapter 21	Acceptance Of Oneself Is Self-Love 255
Chapter 22	Living with Body Dysmorphic Disorder and learning to love oneself... 262

FOREWORD

Ursh Arthars

"I'm all about body positivity and self-love because I believe that we can save the world if we first save ourselves". - Lizzo

Welcome to a book about one of the most crucial subjects of our time: loving oneself.

It can be simple to lose sight of our own worth and value in a world where we are inundated with messages about how we should behave, how we should look, and what we should accomplish. Self-love is the cure for these damaging messages as well as the secret to leading an authentic and happy life.

In this book, you will find inspiring stories and practical advice to help you cultivate a deep and abiding love for yourself. Through the stories shared by each author in this book, you will learn how to let go of self-judgment and embrace your unique strengths and weaknesses. You will discover how setting healthy boundaries, practising self-care, and nourishing your mind, body, and spirit are the secrets to living your best life. And most importantly, you will learn that self-love is not selfish but rather the foundation of all meaningful relationships and accomplishments.

As a self-proclaimed workaholic and perfectionist, I know firsthand the devastating effects of not practising self-love. My journey has been difficult, marked by burnout, chronic fatigue, and an autoimmune condition that has had a negative impact on both my physical and mental health. It was a constant battle for me to put my needs first, but I soon understood that self-love was the secret to my recovery. Without it, I was stuck in a vicious cycle of self-neglect and suffering, but with it, I found the strength and resilience to heal and thrive.

As Mel Robbins says, "The relationship you have with yourself sets the tone for every other relationship you have." By prioritising self-care and self-love, I was able to rebuild and continue to build my relationship with myself. It made it possible for me to free myself from the strangling effects of perfectionism and work addiction and to embrace a more wholesome and genuine way of life. Every day, I continue to benefit from my dedication to loving myself.

The journey towards self-acceptance and personal growth can be challenging. Brene Brown's book, "The Gifts of Imperfection", has taught me to embrace my imperfections and vulnerabilities and to practise self-compassion and gratitude, which has had a profound positive impact on my mental and emotional wellbeing. As Brené Brown said, "Authenticity is the daily practise of letting go of who we think we're supposed to be and embracing who we are."

Finding self-love and healing can be a difficult process. "The Self-Love Experiment" by Shannon Kaiser was instrumental in my recovery. This book helped me to let go of self-doubt and negative self-talk and cultivate a deeper sense of self-worth and self-acceptance. By following her practical and transformative exercises, I have learned to prioritise my needs, practise self-love on a daily basis, rebuild my energy, and prioritise my health and overall well-being. As Mel Robbins said, "Self-love is an ongoing, lifelong journey. It's not a destination, it's a practice."

I am thrilled to be writing the forward for Alicia's third book in her trilogy. I had the pleasure of first meeting Alicia at a Meta Dynamics training in 2018. From the moment we started talking, I could tell that she was a dynamic, driven, and inspiring woman. Her passion for helping others achieve their goals and aspirations was evident, and I knew right away that she was someone special.

Alicia's commitment to collaboration and giving back is evident in all that she does. Her first two books, "Gratitude Journey of the Soul" and "Forgiveness Healing of the Soul", have created opportunities for dozens of coaches, including myself, to share their stories and insights. By doing so, she has not only helped to amplify the voices of others, but she has also created a sense of community and support that is truly remarkable.

I have absolutely no doubt that this third book will be just as inspiring and transformative as the first two. Alicia has a gift for creating a space where people can come together, learn from each other, and grow. I feel honoured to be a part of this journey, and I look forward to seeing how Alicia continues to impact the world of coaching and beyond.

For over 23 years, I've had the honour of transforming thousands of women's lives physically, spiritually, and mentally. From my experience, one truth remains evident: genuine happiness stems from cultivating a positive mindset.

I am the owner of New Zealand's longest-running women's gym, *Results Fitness*, a transformational coach, and the founder of Body by Design, an online emotional eating weight loss program.

My life purpose and passion are to empower and inspire women to cultivate a deep and meaningful relationship with themselves, embrace their strengths and vulnerabilities and practise self-love and self-care on a daily basis. My ultimate goal is to help women live authentically, confidently, and joyfully and to create a positive ripple effect in their personal and professional life.

I have had the privilege of interviewing Alicia and many other incredible women who are achieving genuine success through my podcast, *The Mind Fitness Mentor*. These women's stories serve as inspiring reminders that self-love is a powerful force that can transform lives and facilitate growth in unimaginable ways.

I believe that self-love is the foundation of all positive change, and it is through this lens that I approach my work with clients. By embracing vulnerability and self-love, we can create the space for true transformation and growth.

Whether you are struggling with low self-esteem, dealing with past traumas or burnout, or simply want to deepen your connection with yourself, this book is for you. It is a powerful reminder that you are worthy of love, just as you are. It's time to make self-love a priority and start living your best life.

MIRROR MIRROR ON THE WALL: A LETTER FROM THE EDITOR

Alicia Ann Wade

"Self-Love is a journey, not a destination."

In that instant, I once more despised my reflection when I looked in the mirror.
My life once again came crashing down in August 2021.

How did I lose my identity and fall into the deep, dark hole?
How did I get so lost that I lost everything?
Why did all my accomplishments, including being named Life Coach of the Year, International Best-Selling Author, and Educator of the Year, suddenly come crashing down?

I should have been regarded as successful and content once more, but instead, I sank to the lowest levels of sadness and depression. I felt isolated.

"Success without fulfillment is the ultimate failure." Tony Robbins and I have fallen into the depths of unfulfillment in life again!

In 2021, when I was once more on the verge of near-death experiences, I relapsed and began to binge drink on the weekends. I desperately wanted to numb the excruciating pain I was feeling as a result of being rejected and excluded from groups and collaborations. In the coaching community, it is encouraged for us to speak our truth, tell our story, and take pride in who we are. Nevertheless, I was overthrown in a split second. The pin was pulled 24 hours before a public announcement to run for the Australian Federal Election, and this is where I suffered significant losses. I was left on my own despite investing hundreds of thousands of dollars, having clients pull the pin on me, and being expelled from community groups. In order to hide who I really was and who I had made myself out to be, I masked stories, dismantled articles, and altered my media press releases.

My childhood trauma resurfaced along with that sense of rejection. My old coping mechanisms also made a stronger appearance than ever before.

I engaged in acts I wasn't proud of out of a desire to be loved. Was this love, though? No, I was on a rampage of trying to feel good and loved, but these were just empty temporary fixes like a cocaine addict addicted to the high. The feeling of belonging had vanished from my life so suddenly. People have loved me and hated me for my past, which is publicly available through Amazon. I've also received praise and insults from people. In particular from my published book BE-OUTSTANDING: 5 Simple Steps to Turn Your Life's Mess to Success!

What Does it Mean to Me to Love Myself?

I've been researching and I am pursuing a master's degree in Applied Positive Psychology. To value, accept, and care for oneself is to practise self-love. It entails treating oneself kindly, compassionately, and understandingly as well as appreciating one's value as a person and realising one's worth. It also includes taking responsibility for one's happiness and well-being and making choices that align with one's values and needs. Self-love involves more than just feeling good about oneself; it also entails taking care of oneself in a way that promotes overall wellbeing and a fulfilling life.

I had not been able to do this until this very moment. In my life, something needed to change at the end of 2022. My reputation among people is one of great success and total success. Nevertheless, because I am a human, I am going through my own human experiences of self-awareness and discovery.

I founded *The Gratitude Method TM*; this was a major focus in 2021 and I realised that this was the saviour to my life and self-sabotaging behaviours that had brought me to the verge of death. In 2022, I finished my 365 days of gratitude, and even though a relapse was taking place in the background, it ultimately taught me to be grateful for the things in my life.

I did the unthinkable in March of 2022. When I was engaged in an immoral act, I was embarrassed and ashamed. It was at this point I realised that I needed to stop my behaviour and accept responsibility for everything that had happened up until this point.

In collaboration with 24 other incredible authors, Forgiveness Healing of the Soul was born there. As they shared their triumphs and tragedies with me, I realised that I was also on a healing journey. I describe a path to self-forgiveness in the book, and I came to the realisation that this is where we are right now. The time has come for me to love myself more than what I have done for my mind, body, and spirit because I am practicing gratitude every day. I have forgiven myself.

How do you practice self-love in your daily life?

Since my first mental breakdown in 2015, I have been on a massive happiness journey. Self-love is a journey, not a destination. I realised that practicing self-love does not involve exhausting yourself in the gym twice or three times a day while believing that you are doing it for your health. Self-love is not limiting yourself to the foods you enjoy. I was exhibiting an unhealthy form of fitness, and I was also exhibiting another form of addiction. In the past four years, I've was vegan, and I've also learned to love food rather than feel bad about eating or having a hearty meal. In order to burn off the calories, I see a lot of women either feel guilty or work out vigorously. I too was one of those women. I read Marianne Williamson's book "A Course in Weight Loss," and it was there that I learned how to make mealtimes a ritual, be grateful, and enjoy every bite without feeling guilty or bad about myself. Everything changes when we eat with intention, intuition, and love.

After my second breakdown, I realised that the itty-bitty pity party was back in full force. The mirror has also reestablished itself as not a friend. I realised I had rubbed off all the "I am" affirmations in my bedroom for more than a year. They have since gone back up and here is the list:

I am loved
I am enough
I am confident
I am successful
I am fun
I am loving
I am kind
I am wise
I am a learning machine
I am knowledgeable
I am present
I am awesome
I am the BEST
I am unique
I am ME
I am ALICIA
2AW
NEXT LEVEL

I read this every day in my room, and my calendar also notifies me of events at 8 a.m., 12 p.m., and 4 p.m. I AM LOVED, I AM GROWING, I AM INDEPENDENT, I AM SEXY. This has been playing for more than two years, serving as a reminder to put the negative thoughts in the past. I suppose this kept me here on an unconscious level.

In what ways do you believe society impacts an individual's ability to love themselves?

It is so difficult to make sense of social media, news, professionals, experts, celebrities, and other information that's available everywhere. It can be confusing because so many things have an impact on us, including veganism, carnivore diets, trying to look a certain way, plastic surgery, cool sculpting, altering your body, and changing sex. Since then, I have turned off the news. I haven't watched TV or movies, and I don't even have a TV in my room. I conduct my own research based on interest or science, in accordance with my morals, spiritual beliefs, and values. There is so much to take in that deciding where to focus your energy is entirely up to you. Don't hold back if it makes you happier. If it has a negative effect on you, eliminate it from your life and move on. This life and the world already have enough going on for you to add more to it.

How do you believe self-love is related to mental and physical well-being?

Self-love is directly related to both mental and physical health; when you accept yourself, you develop self-love; when you forgive yourself, you develop self-love; and when you are thankful, you develop self-love. These straightforward but effective qualities and strengths will alter your reality.

The photos you see today on my social media and the latest bikini shoot with Mariah Creative Photography are of myself and who I am after years of conflict with my reflection in the mirror. I continue to get the nicknames "big butt" and "fat" from some people even though others think I look happy, healthy, and fit. What matters most is how you come to accept who you are and what you do to better yourself. I packed on 20kgs in the last year due to illnesses, past partners calling me names and being rejected. The use of food as comfort followed, along with the use of alcohol, poor eating habits, and occasionally excessive exercise. Thus, my body did not receive the care it required. It received punishment every single day. Your soul is nurtured when your body is. I'm telling you right now that I'm trying to accept and be kind to myself. After my photo shoot, I finally let go of my tendency to judge myself and beat myself up, which made it possible for me to embrace every aspect of my female body. Thanks to Mariah Lee Creative, I was able to overcome any demons I had by bringing such joy and love to the photoshoot. I have been anorexic, overeating, obese and masculine. I feel more feminine now than I ever have. I work out every day, and I never skip more than two weeks. I've kept up my fitness and health for eight years. As I turn 40 in 2023, just before the release of this book, I've learned to love my curves rather than despise or punish myself for not having more or less than what I already have!

Story time...

I was the only "Fat Kid," and I couldn't help but love food. It was delicious then, and it still is. However, in retrospect, I realise that the number of packaged snacks I consumed—such as chips, candy, chocolate, processed foods, meat, and dairy—was not healthy. Growing up, I was a difficult child who would cry out in protest if I wasn't given what I wanted to eat. My poor mother had to put up with my cravings for unhealthy foods! I was called things like "fatty boom-sticks" and "Miss. Piggy," and those things stuck with me and haunted me as a child. I was probably seven or eight years old at the time. Once more, the circumstances of the time mould us for later life. Getting my balance back has required a lot of healing, self-love, and care. I, therefore, balance the food today. To relieve the stress of "forcing" or "not enjoying" the act of eating, I eat healthfully and intuitively.

In year 2, we were asked to weigh ourselves in class, going from heaviest to lightest. This information was then displayed on a fishing wire that ran across the room, making it visible to everyone. I was the third-heaviest student in the class and the heaviest girl. Here is where my thoughts and I were really impacted by the conditioning of numbers and scale weight. This is where my focus on the scales to get the ideal weight came from. But what is the perfect number? I now try to avoid doing it and only weigh myself once a month, as doing so lessens the obsessiveness and old ways of controlling my life.

Let's move on to year three, where communication between peers had gotten worse. I can still picture a game called "Hospitals" being played. Everyone was given roles by a particular girl, and I was given the part of the "pillow blob" because I was fat, had a soft stomach, and the patients in the imaginative play game could lie on my stomach rather than the playground cement. 'Pillow Blob!' Another hit to my self-confidence and a reminder of how fat I was, shaming me even more than ever. The patient would say, "Oh wow, pillow blob, you are so soft and comfy!" In my head, I thought, thanks for telling me how fat I am! Appreciate it! Hats off for really defining me, even more, letting me know how fat I am and shaming me further.

As you can see, there were a lot of emotions and hurt from this, but I have overcome this, and I know what to do to feel good.

Let's move on to high school, where it became even more difficult to adjust due to language and meaning's increased potency. I experienced the 'fat' shame again in years seven and eight. I remember a situation from netball. I was the goal defence and was performing at the top of my game until a teammate girl yelled, "Oh my god! Just look at you! You are so fat you have a hole in your dress!" I did have a hole, but I didn't know how to sew, and the threading had come loose. Once more, I looked in the mirror while sobbing, despising who I was, and desiring to disappear or to be only thin. Words cannot express the emotions I experienced when I looked in the mirror or the thoughts of hating who I was. My entire childhood was spent being teased, which left me feeling unloved and lacking in confidence. It was difficult, and until I was in my 20s or possibly 30s, I never talked about it. Suppressed feelings, hurt, sadness, and depression are just a few of the emotions that I've written down to describe how I was feeling. I used to slap, punch, and pull my skin off of my body and attempt to rip it off because I hated and loathed who I was.

These are just a few of the tales I tell in my book, "BE-Outstanding." The mirror has been a useful tool in helping me get past this, and daily I AM affirmations are what keep those demons inside my head at bay.

Remember that self-love is a journey, not a destination, and that you cannot say, "I've arrived at self-love, and that's it." DONE, TICK, NEXT. It is a daily practice for your own personal development; you will learn more about yourself and become more conscious of your next course of action. Since you are your only rival, challenge yourself daily to find ways to make yourself happy. It is a journey towards contentment, fulfilment, and happiness.

Relationships with others and the value of self-love. I have a very cliche saying, "love yourself and others will love you too." I used to say, "I hate the world and the world hates me". So, you can only see how my world was created. Create an environment of love, happiness, and joy around you. To experience life more positively, you simply need to put the techniques I'll be teaching you into practice. Continue reading. You will become even more aware of happiness and purpose as a result.

You must take action to practise self-love. By following the steps below, you will learn how to incorporate this practice into your daily activities and way of life. Find a professional or coach to assist you, whether it be a health coach, life coach, or spiritual coach, and ask them to assist you in putting new self-love strategies into practice. Or even better, enrol in self-help courses, programmes, or workshops that interest you to gain more information, resources, and tools to enrich your life.

There is a wealth of information available on how to practise self-love, so even if you don't feel like it, make it a daily habit! You will notice the effects it has on your mind, body, and spirit over the long run, and it will benefit you.

Practice self-care:

Make sure to take care of your physical and emotional needs daily. This can involve engaging in physical activity, eating healthfully, getting enough sleep, and setting aside time to unwind and relax. Keep in mind that you are not depriving yourself when you eat and exercise. It wasn't until I learned and became more aware of the fact that I was carrying out all these actions for the wrong reasons that I stopped wondering why so many coaches and health professionals talk about this. Exercise was an addiction, eating became obsessive, relaxing (well, this never happened). So, take a look at your calendar and schedule everything appropriately. Time Blocking ensures that everything gets done! All tasks are time-blocked and completed! Your day will be better spent because of it.

Set boundaries:

Learn to say no to things and people that don't serve you, and make time for the things that do. I used to have a coaching motto: "Say YES and figure out how." but that caused a breakdown because I am a recovering people-pleaser. If it frightens you, that doesn't mean you should ignore your fear and proceed. Ask yourself honestly if the task aligns with your values, interests, purpose, vision, and mission. This was one of the biggest learning lessons in my life! Be mindful of coaching jargon and the personal development community; both can be toxic and cause negative outcomes.

Speak kindly to yourself:

Be mindful of the language you use when thinking and speaking to yourself. Practice speaking and writing in a positive, inspiring manner. Use **I AM** affirmations on the wall, schedule events on your phone with three daily reminders, write **I AM** affirmations in a journal, and then ask yourself what self-love means, feels, and looks like for you. Drop into embodiment or meditation fully and enjoy yourself!

Forgive yourself:

We all make mistakes. Learn to let go of the past and put your attention on the future. It took me 38 years to realise how to be kinder to myself and that I could only know what I knew at that point in time in my timeline. Be understanding because you can only know what is happening right now and what you have learned and experienced up to this point. As you gain more self-awareness, change your course but don't stop trying to get better and advance in life.

Surround yourself with positivity:

Spend time with people who uplift and support you, and limit your exposure to negativity. After being bullied for most of my formative years, I've learned another lesson that I share with many people: my best friends are my best friends because they encourage me, stand by me, and only want the best for me as I do for them. These can probably be counted on one hand. Keep them nearby! Eliminate the remainder! Block them everywhere, even better.

Show yourself compassion:

Treat yourself with the same kindness and understanding that you would show to a friend. Mirror-gaze and pay attention to your inner voice. I have a series of questions I ask my inner critic, and I learned from my mentor and use it with my clients too:

STEPS TO MANAGE YOUR "INNER CRITIC

Step 1
Notice the critic
What are you saying to yourself in the mirror?
What are you saying to your reflection?

Step 2
Separate the critic from you.

Step 3
Talk back.

Step 4
Replace the critic!

Then take the time to reflect:

- Is this an old story playing out in my life?
- Have I heard this before?
- What would I get for buying this story?
- Could this be helpful, or is my mind babbling on?
- Does this thought help me take effective action?
- Am I going to trust my mind or my experience?

Another great resource is mirror work by Lousie Hay. I highly recommend it to those who still have a horrible inner critic.

Something to ponder on, if you were to hear how you treat yourself in your head, I bet it would be WORSE than a domestic violence relationship. So, why is it not okay to be in a DV relationship and okay to be horrible to yourself? Take responsibility for your thoughts and uplift yourself.

Watch your relationships in your reality change as a result of this work! ♥

♥ BE KIND

♥ LOVE YOURSELF

♥ AND BRING THAT TO OTHER'S LIVES TOO

♥ WE ALL SHOULD FEEL AND EXPERIENCE LOVE ♥

Prioritise self-discovery:

Take the time to learn about yourself, your values, and your needs. I also advise doing this if it involves hiring a life coach, counselling, attending a personal development seminar, or seeing a professional. Hire a coach to assist you in learning more. They can challenge you and probably see more ways to aid in your self-discovery. You'd be asked questions you've never thought to ask yourself, or even better, learn new things at the conference that you can apply to your life.

Practice spirituality:

Whatever you believe in, have some sort of spiritual practice. I now attend church on a weekly basis to receive encouragement, learn how to live and lead with love, prayer daily, rosary prayer and have my cup refilled. My relationship with God has made it possible for me to improve my relationship with myself, which has a knock-on effect on my family and friends. I've had many bigger-scale encounters with love. The Holy Spirit's love is what has also saved me. The church and the strength of this community has allowed for my awakening and my attendance at numerous retreats, breathwork sessions, and sound healing sessions has helped me find my heart and love once more. Find the community you're looking for there, too! We are loved and we belong! We are beautiful and unique because God, higher power, made us that way!

Allow yourself to make mistakes:

It's okay to not have all the answers or to make mistakes. Allow yourself to grow and learn from your experiences. Give up trying to be in control or perfect. I believe that if a project or task is 80% finished, it is acceptable because you are only comparing it to your own standards in life. People will compliment you, so use those words of encouragement to push forwards and keep following your path.

Set achievable goals:

Create short and long-term goals for yourself, and work towards achieving them. Set 5–10-year ones you will be surprised at how they come to life! I made some goals five years ago, and they have all been realised. Despite the fact that I am in the dating world for the right reasons and am very clear about what I want in a partner, I am only looking for one person—a life partner. Additionally, I recently developed the "Your BEST Year Yet" Programme using the 777 rule: 7 tasks, 7 days plan on the 7th day for the week ahead and watch your world change!

For more information see: https://www.thegratitudemethod.com/yourbestyearyet

Practice gratitude:

Take time each day to reflect on what you are grateful for in your life. Additionally, list 10 reasons why you are grateful for your body. This was the most difficult thing I have ever done. When I was asked to do this. I couldn't even think of 1, now I am able to list off so many and this is where the power and magic is! I appreciate Ursh Arthars, my health coach, for teaching me this only a year ago! I'm a big proponent of gratitude, and this was on another level!

Visit: www.thegratitudemethod.com to see my books and products to help you practise gratitude! I also have several journals and products in this category.

In what ways do you believe self-love can positively impact the world around us?

If everyone incorporates self-love into their lifestyle, the world will change. I believe this to be a superpower, and the work that is being done today would not be necessary if everyone loved themselves more. Eliminating mental health is likely to happen! It is time to spread the word about these practices in order to reduce the 1 in 2 statistics of people who experience mental illness in their lifetime. Mental Health is real and raw! If you put these tips into practice, you can overcome depression and anxiety. To overcome this and bring about a world filled with joy, love, happiness, and gratitude, I'm on a mission! Together, we can accomplish this!

I want to finish off with a Self-Love prayer that is in my Soul Sisters Sonia Raco Journal "I am Enough"

A Self-Love Prayer

Mother Mother, send your angels to guide and protect my mind, body and spirit.

Direct me in every single step to fulfil my divine destiny.

Let there be your favour, upon favour over my life, relationships, career and family.

Heal my past, help me embrace my present and to feel excited for my future.

Love me in all the ways that I may struggle to love myself.

Amen

So, remember Self-Love is a journey, not a destination.

CHAPTER 1

What is the Ratio you spend on Life's obligations compared to time spent on self-love?

Rhonda Dodds

"Loving oneself is like breathing; it is necessary, and we should be doing it without thought."

How do you define self-love? Self-love /self'ləv/noun regard for one's well-being and happiness (chiefly considered as a desirable rather than narcissistic characteristic).

Self-love is a state of appreciation for oneself that grows from actions that support our physical, psychological, and spiritual growth. Self-love means having a high regard for your well-being and happiness, and self-love means taking care of your needs and not sacrificing your well-being to please others.

I look at the definition of self-love and wonder how I can take action to preserve my happiness while being raised to always take care of others. My mother and father worked many hours; I was seven and eight years older than my two baby sisters, and I made dinner, helped clean, and entertained my littles. My childhood is a story for another day, but I will say that when a child is in fear of consequences from a parent that looks for any fault to heap them upon you, one becomes a people-pleaser at all costs. It would have been nice to mirror self-love instead of accidentally finding it later.

If you are a person who always says yes, ask yourself these three questions: Feel free to write the answers in the margins of the book; if you don't want to write in books like me, a notebook or an app on your phone will work just fine. If you feel ready, you can begin the journaling journey now. Make it genuine; write it down.

1. When you agree to help someone, is it because you want to, because you think they will be mad at you if you say no, or maybe you don't feel that you have a choice and the only answer is yes?

2. What is (insert your name here)'s definition of self-love?

3. According to the stage of life you are currently going through, self-love changes. Since every reader is a different age, I ask you to divide your current age into four sections. Then, consider each of those periods in your life and identify what self-love meant to you at that time. Mine, for instance, would be 14, 28, 42, and 57.

I chose to do some research on people-pleasing because I had some concerns.

What is the definition of a people-pleaser?

The term "people pleaser" refers to a person who has a strong urge to please others, even if at their own expense. They may feel that their wants and needs do not matter or alter their personalities around others. Wow, talk about the opposite of self-love!

Is it bad to say yes to people? Not a simple yes or no question, and being a good person is different than saying yes when we want to say no. According to studies, the consequences of being a people-pleaser driven by a fear of saying no are quite negative. After reading about the cost that pleasing people could have on my health, I would have to compare it to thinking of my time as a bank account with minutes instead of money. What is my balance? How am I spending my time? Since I won't be able to get it back, how should I spend my time to ensure that it was well spent and brought me happiness? Let's start with the motivators for pleasing others.

What makes a person a people-pleaser?

According to the numerous articles I've read, learning to please people starts in early life. A child's awareness of danger may be increased by a birth illness, a traumatic experience as a child, or by mirroring an adult. People-pleasers may want to stay safe or prevent a tense situation from going into overdrive. People-pleasers need to feel loved, safe and accepted. I could list other abuses or traumatic events that can cause insecurity in your life so much that you must ensure everyone is happy. No matter who it is—whether it's a new acquaintance or a member of your immediate family—you have been programmed to assist.

What are the signs of a people-pleaser?

You say sorry way too often.
You will do anything to avoid disagreement.
When someone doesn't like you, you feel devastated.
You are usually the one at a gathering who makes sure everyone is happy.
Saying no makes you sad and guilty, leaving you searching for ways to make it work.
You don't ask for help when it's needed because you don't want to bother others.
You won't share your hurt feelings with someone else because you don't want them upset with you.
You are overloaded with validation responsibilities due to taking on favours for others and your own tasks.
You often look for validation from your friends and family in your choices to make you feel secure in yourself.

I am not a professional, but if you need more help than what self-help can provide, I strongly advise finding a good therapist. A skilled expert who, in these circumstances, is equipped with the tools to assist in rebuilding a different reaction than the damaged one we repeatedly give. If you are uncomfortable leaving your home to talk to a therapist, recently the ways we can receive professional help have expanded to include Zoom or even a phone call. Refrain from allowing the cost, time, and location to hold you back. You are worth it, and once you try, you'll learn how a therapist will work with your budget.

What effects can PP manifest?

Lack of self-love and neglecting one's own needs
You find it hard to have a good time because you constantly observe others waiting to meet their needs.
You find yourself stressed and anxious due to being overly stimulated, which makes it hard to wind down.
Passive aggressive behaviour is brought on by pent-up resentment from anger or frustration.
find it difficult to decide because of self-doubt.
Weakens or cultivates unhealthy relationships that are out of balance.
When you pull inward rather than express your feelings to others, communication can break down.
Harmful stress affects the body and mind negatively.
You are under pressure to always be gracious and upbeat.
You lose yourself because you are always busy taking care of others.
Frustration from your needs not being fulfilled.

How does a people-pleaser say no?

In all my research, it comes down to loving yourself enough to say no. My intention is not to make you feel as if you should have just known the answer. Once we have the tools we need, it gets easier.

Self-love for me

I described in the chapter's introduction how I developed a people-pleasing personality. It turned into a coping strategy; I was unaware that what I was doing had a name. I didn't realise that until I was nearing the end of my forties and had symptoms other than rheumatoid arthritis. Now I have to look after myself! I quickly became too exhausted to do anything. Due to the overwhelming nature of life, I started to resent helping others and developed a bad attitude. I required balance. I realised then that something needed to change. I tend to be very upbeat and optimistic, so I didn't want to lose myself in the idea that everything needed to be handled before me. I researched podcasts, hygge, yoga, and much more, and I have discovered a beautiful word for what I have always needed. Self-love. Let me explain how it functions for me. Once again, I sat down and wrote down all my obligations.

When my obligations to myself become clear, I'll divide the list into daily, weekly, and monthly tasks that I want to share. I had a craving for my Ah May Zing go-to comfort soup. The time I spent preparing compared to the time I spent enjoying my Ah May Zing Potato Go-to Comfort Soup was an eye-opener. Cooking is one of my favourite calming activities. My goal is to create a YUM moment. I like the smell of ingredients changing individually in simmering soup. The soup takes two hours from start to finish. After getting comfortable, grabbing a blanket, and starting a movie, I scooped up my steaming bowl of chunky potato soup, topped with bacon, cheddar cheese, and cracked pepper; I settled in. The soup with hot bread and butter tasted incredible.

I am not trying to make the responsibilities of life sound awful. I would write a different chapter and not value self-love as much as I do if we had more self-love than obligations. I am trying to make the analogy that you might have a full day of life that needs to be completed. Take the time to enjoy yourself for an hour at some point in the day, every day!

I'm currently fifty-seven. My RA is in good shape. Following some self-help, back to the list of gotta-dos" I started. Self-love time must be scheduled specifically in your schedule. At least in the beginning. I figured that, like daily tasks, self-love must be intentional. For example, I do three things every morning: brewing the coffee, making the bed, and laying out my clothes for the next day. I do not have to put these in the to-do slots anymore. I became so practised in what needed to be done that every morning I completed my list without having to look at it. This doesn't make my life robotic; it makes it less stressful and more natural. I feel it and know something is missing if I arrive late and haven't made my bed. After you start scheduling a daily slot, even if it only lasts for fifteen minutes at first and you end up working an hour, that is what self-love will turn into for you. Anything longer than an hour, in my opinion, is a plus!

What does my self-love time every night look like? I have it in the bag! No, I have a self-love bag. The two reasons it is a self-love bag are that I need it to be mobile. Suppose I want to be in the living room to watch TV with my husband or go out in my shed. I even take my self-love bag on vacation. Two, I have a variety of choices because my OCD won't let me be disorganised. At that time in my life, I could do anything I wanted to. The contents of the bag are entirely about me. I enjoy something from the bag every night. My methods of self-love will evolve along with life. There would be a pause in the constant fear and anxiety in my belly to let either parent know I was helping, listening, and sucking up to either parent. And so, without giving it a name, the great discovery that makes me feel better and temporarily placed those who are angry with me begins.

In trying to consolidate my life journey to get you to the self-love I enjoy every day, I decided to answer the third question I asked you earlier.

In a different way than it had in my early years, self-love was saying yes to me when I was fourteen through seventeen. I would latch on to any male attention given to me, and I found myself in many relationships that only benefited the other person. I would let people walk all over me. Attention is attention, right? I cared for myself in vain, ensuring I did my hair and makeup daily. Only if I looked my best would I leave the house. I wasn't going to give anyone a chance to make fun of me. But I didn't feel my best at the end of most days.

I had a husband, two daughters, and a lovely family by the time I was twenty-eight. To me, self-love meant making sure I had taken care of my family, the house was clean, and everything had a place, and it was my responsibility to get it there at the end of the day. I was the OCD ninja; if a cup was left out, I was there to take it home. I loved my baby girls and still do with all my heart. Let me go back a little bit. Before the birth of my second daughter, I was aware that I couldn't quit because we needed the money from my job. I missed my daughter, and I wanted to be the one to raise her. I love children and have always been more comfortable around them than adults. Honestly, I still am! I opened a daycare in my home and loved my life.

I also added teaching Sunday school for many years to my schedule after the birth of my second daughter. I discovered crochet during my first pregnancy and rediscovered it during my second. I remember sitting down with a crochet project after the house was clean and falling asleep before I could crochet a stitch. I was exhausted and needed to sleep to give myself all I had the next day. I gave all I had, but did I give the best?

Up until my 42nd year, a lot of life events occurred. I took a job at the neighbourhood hospital because my daughters were in full-time school. I soon realised that I had a lot of free time at night and began to feel uneasy. I tried taking on numerous hobbies, working a second job waitressing, teaching crochet at the college, etc., but I was never content. I paid attention to the fact that I could never sit still at night. I had no problem feeling fulfilled when caring for people at the hospital during the day. I was curious as to why whenever I wasn't busy, I experienced anxiety. I made a list of all my responsibilities and when I completed them. I still had open nights. The first step in establishing a time to unwind at night was to have open time slots.

I initially learned to crochet, but I had to recognise it for what it was. Self-love. My mind never stopped working. I was always searching for something to keep me busy or calm me.

At the end of the chapter, I have included a self-love bag recipe and my Ah May Zing potato soup recipe. I pray all who read this book find peace and suggestions that help them.

If you want to chat with me or have any questions, contact me at startingover2daze@gmail.com.

Loving oneself is like breathing; it is necessary, and we should be doing it without thought. -Rhonda Dodds-

Self-Love Bag recipe (I have added suggestions to help you have ideas if needed)

Comfy clothes
I write this acronym on the front of my journals:

S-Self Advocate, say no.
E-Evaluate each situation and take time to answer.
L-Love yourself first; there is only one you.
F-Focus on your needs.
L-Laugh Often.
O-Optimize your self-love time by being prepared.
V-Visualize yourself in peace.
E-Emerge a better person.

Start with creating a comfort agenda, journal, or daily tasks with a slot for self-love.
I use Bogg Bags https://boggbag.com/.
I have a Spanish notebook/fun pen (I am currently learning Spanish). Duolingo is the app.
My Current Crochet projects.
Notebook and Pen to practise penmanship
Prayer Journal (leather with Deckle edge paper from Amazon)
Planner (Tools4wisdom planner from Amazon)
Word search
Current book I am reading.
Ear pods to listen to crime shows on Spotify, or a book on Audible.
Charging cord and portable charger

Self-Love

Ah May Zing Potato Soup

Ingredients:
3 tbsp butter or olive oil
2 Cups diced carrots.
1 Large onion-chopped
2 Large garlic cloves peeled and diced.
4 tbsp flour
1 heaping tbsp Knorr tomato bouillon.
6 Large potatoes Peeled and cut in half, then into one-inch chunks.
3 Cups chicken broth
2 cups water
2 Cups chopped bacon split into 1 cup for soup, 1 cup for topping.
3 Cups half and half
3 Cups shredded cheddar cheese or smoked Gouda divided into 1 cup for soup, and 2 cups for topping.
Pinch of salt
Potato masher or inversion blender
1 Med sweet onion diced for topping.
Cracked pepper for topping.

Directions:

Add 3 tbsp butter or olive oil, 2 cups diced carrots, a large, chopped onion, and two large garlic cloves in a large soup pot. Sauté for three minutes on high, stirring every 30 seconds.

Add 4 tbsp flour and one heaping tbsp Knorr tomato bouillon coating sauteed ingredients.

Add Potato chunks, 3 cups chicken broth, and 2 cups water. Bring to a boil, then drop down to a simmer for 25 minutes stirring several times.

When potatoes can be pierced easily with a fork, use a potato masher or inversion blender to mash down half the potatoes.

Add bacon, 3 cups half and half, 1 cup of cheese, and a pinch of salt. Simmer until hot. Remove from heat.

Finish by topping soup bowls with bacon, cheese, sweet onion, and cracked pepper.

Warm bread and sweet butter are a great addition to this delicious soup.

If you feel the soup isn't thick enough, heat two tbsp of butter or olive oil in a small pan, stir in 2 tbsp flour, add to soup, and stir till thick.

CHAPTER 2

An Idle Tuesday Afternoon

Deleine Gavin-Cox

"Self-love may not happen overnight, but be kind and patient with yourself."

I saw the missed calls. I re-contacted my stepbrother and enquired, "Is she still alive?" He replied, "No, I'm so sorry, but your mother just passed away," sighing and clearly in tears.

Have you ever felt so engulfed in suffering and hurt? Feeling anger, confusion, grief, and that your soul is just broken? I was 23 years old and on the fast track to failure. I indulged in destructive behaviour, binge drinking, toxic relationships, partying, and yo-yo dieting to dull my pain.Unfortunately, these things caused more pain, feeding my inner critic's belief that I was not good enough and that I was alone. I did not love myself at all.

I had a difficult start to life, beginning with the death of my father when I was just three years old. He was struck by a truck as we crossed a road. A heartbreaking decision to end my father's life had to be made six weeks later by my mother, who had two young daughters under four and severe mental health issues. I cannot remember any of these events, but growing up, there were many moments when my mother would blame me for my father's death. Her pain made her lash out at me, and my being around caused my mother's pain to intensify. As a result, my Nan took me in to live with her for nearly a year. Living with my Nan was the best time of my life. She was kind and loving, and I was her princess.

In contrast, when I returned to live at home with my mum, who had remarried by this time, I was met with a mixture of love, hate, and, at times, abuse in different forms. My mother's erratic mental health and my complex relationship with my stepfather meant that being home was not always a great place for me. There were times when I would be sent to live with a family member or, at times, in foster care. Unfortunately, moving from Melbourne to Mildura meant that living with Nan was not an option. No matter where I was, I felt like an outsider and never quite fit in. I carried this feeling of self-loathing throughout my childhood and into adulthood. The relationship with my mother and stepfather was emotionally draining. I constantly fought for their attention and love, yet I felt anger and sadness towards them. Years later, I would understand that my mother's mental health condition and my stepfather's trauma caused them to treat me the way they did, which was a reflection of them.

You have probably heard the stories of how destructive self-hatred is, and my life was very much lived this way. I attracted friends who didn't share my core values, and we often got into trouble due to shoplifting or some other petty offence, but I didn't care. I was happy to adjust my opinions or behaviour to please anyone who showed an ounce of interest in me. I would pretend to be interested in whatever they were, even if it went against everything I believed in. I was quite the chameleon because, at the heart of it, I just wanted anyone in my life to love me. Consequently, many would realise this and exit my life in a blaze of chaos.

Throughout school, I was bullied, which contributed to my self-perceived lack of worth and inability to fit in. I transitioned from destructive friendships to domestically violent relationships and ended up at a point where I just wanted to end my life. It was a never-ending cycle; through it, I pretended that I was confident and self-assured, and I had moments where I believed I was. As I entered adulthood, I started reconciling with my mother and stepfather, and I made friends more aligned with who I was. I was also fortunate to have found a good job with a great boss. Even so, I still felt deeply unhappy within myself. I would often wonder, how everyone else had life all figured out. I resigned myself to believing that I would always be a complete mess, and then that fateful Tuesday happened.

It was an Idle Tuesday afternoon and day two of my new job. I had just ended a meeting with my new boss and felt the urge to check my phone. In those days, you didn't check your phone; it was not proper work etiquette, but I did anyway. When I did, I was shocked to discover numerous missed calls and messages from my stepbrother and an unidentified number. I immediately called him, and he sounded upset. What was going on, I questioned him. He told me that my mother and his father (my mother had divorced my stepdad and remarried again) had gone shopping; it was just another regular day, and she needed to go to the bathroom. When someone went in to check on her 15 minutes later because she hadn't emerged, she collapsed. She was taken urgently to a hospital. Mum was relatively healthy aside from asthma, a recent knee operation, and the usual pains of ageing. When I spoke to her a few days earlier, she said she had been feeling good, so there was no reason to suspect this would be too serious. However, for some reason, I didn't ask my stepbrother if she was okay; I asked if she was alive. The next moments were surreal; my heart was racing and my head was pounding as I waited for the answer. He responded with a sigh and obvious tears, "No, I am so sorry, but your mum has just passed away". The upcoming weeks looked so bleak, but I knew I had to persevere. I had to be the one to break the news to my sister, inform our mother's family and friends, deal with her funeral, and come to terms with the fact that I could not recall the last time I had seen or spoken to our mother.

That moment in time, through all the grief, guilt, suffering, and mixed emotions, was the catalyst for the beginning of my self-love journey. Losing Mum so suddenly made me realise that our time on earth could end at any moment. So, the question I asked myself was, "Do I want to spend the rest of my life letting my past story dictate my present and future? No, I didn't.

Suddenly, I had a fire in my belly, unlike anything I had felt before. I looked around me and saw beautiful, happy, and successful people around me, and I wanted what they had. So I made it my mission to learn as much as possible from people around me who had the qualities I aspired to have. I listened to podcasts, read books and surrounded myself with inspirational people. The more I learned, the more I realised that the secret to their happiness came from within. They all had one thing in common: they believed in themselves. They continued to invest in themselves because they had self-acceptance and self-love.

Self-acceptance and kindness: I have found that after a lifetime of self-hatred and loathing, developing self-love is a continuous journey that requires kindness and self-acceptance. Reflecting on my journey, practising self-love is one of the most essential skills that I have learned. I used to look for external validation everywhere. When I didn't get that, I would fall back into feelings of unworthiness. I did, however, come to the realisation that you can only hope for others to love and accept you for who you are if you feel that way yourself.

It was no irony that the final stage of acceptance in the Kubler-Ross Grief Model aligns with finding true self-love. I didn't realise it at the time, but as I went through the stages of grieving over the trauma in my past, including my mother's passing, I was also laying the groundwork for self-acceptance and, ultimately, self-love.

Being kind to yourself and unwaveringly accepting both your positive and negative traits are key components of self-acceptance. The self-love work started once I was able to accept myself as I was, flaws and all. Part of self-acceptance requires you to stop comparing yourself with others and not let other people's opinions of you slow your journey down. You have the freedom and confidence to decide what makes you happy when you don't let other people's opinions or ideas rule your life.

Along the way, I have made a lot of mistakes (although I prefer to think of them as self-imposed life lessons), and occasionally, I have reverted to old habits. This is because I found the change that was taking place to be unsettling. This will happen to you, too, as your inner critic tries to protect you from the unknown, but take a breath, allow yourself to be vulnerable, and see that as a superpower. Allow yourself to make mistakes, embrace your past, and know that you are growing from who you once were into who you are today. You can overcome these obstacles and carry on with your self-love journey with self-compassion and kindness. Recognising your flaws helps you get back on track and serves as a reminder that you should love yourself.

Taking accountability and surrounding yourself with great people - I had a few good friends until I was in my early 20s. Sadly, the unhealthy and toxic relationships were all I could see and think about. I saw myself as a victim, and most people would agree that I was a victim. I was a victim of bullying, I was a victim of domestic violence, and I was a victim of a tough upbringing. So, when I started on my self-love journey, I decided to remove myself from everyone I had surrounded myself with and move to Canada. I would tell people that I would explore the world, as I loved travelling but wanted to escape because I thought changing the place I lived in and the people I was around would change me. It was important to me to own my journey and do something important to me, so I saw this as a wonderful expression of self-love.

I had always dreamed of living abroad but was so stuck in pain or trying to please others that I couldn't even imagine doing this. Moving to Canada gave me freedom like I had never felt before. I felt truly free to be me, which was terrific for the first time in my life. I was no longer bound by the restrictions I had placed on myself and was simply existing. So, it was a massive shock to my system to realise that I was attracting the circumstances of my life. This epiphany dawned on me as I chatted with a new friend in Vancouver over a glass of wine about my life experiences. She was passionate about sharing her experiences with others because she had travelled a similar path as I had. She gave me some book recommendations on awareness and presence exercises as well as the law of attraction. I had always been open to spirituality, so the concept of the law of attraction was not unfamiliar. Nevertheless, two quotes really resonated with me, and I was shocked to discover that I was drawing the people and circumstances in my life to me. These quotes are: "It is not what you want that you attract; you attract what you believe to be true" (Neville Goodhard) and "Whatever is going on in your mind, you are attracting to you" (Bob Proctor).

Initially, I found it difficult to accept that my mindset could attract negative events my life such as bullying, toxic relationships and domestic violence. But as I reflected I realised that I had been living life with a victim mindset and it was holding me back in attracting the right people into my life. My career was a good example of where I had used my mindset to attract positivity. Learning this was just as empowering as self-acceptance. I came to understand that I was in charge of my fate and that it was up to me to bring about the change.

Your vibe attracts your tribe. This quote was famously said by Amy Lee, and how powerful is that statement when you realise you can change it just by practising self-love?

I decided I needed to take responsibility and accountability for changing my vibe. I focused on seeking help, working through my fears, and letting go of the past and toxic people in my life. I realised I needed help to do this. I sought help from a completely impartial counsellor, which was the best thing I have ever done. There are still times when I will reach out and book a session with my counsellor.

It is like a feel-good top-up. I also have a fantastic health coach who has recently been part of my journey.

Gratitude is a powerful tool for changing your vibe and practising self-love. One of the most basic yet effective tools you have at your disposal, gratitude is a game-changer. You'll gain perspective from being grateful, and joy can only be found with gratitude's aid. I keep a daily gratitude journal. I make it a habit to fill it out at the end of the day before I go to bed and re-read it in the morning, so I start and end my day filled with thanks. My mood and vibe are improved by this. If I ever forget to practise gratitude, I notice a difference; negativity can creep in, and the ability to get back on track is more challenging. The great thing is that it is simple to start mindfully practising gratitude again.

I am so fortunate to always be in the company of amazing people. As I focus on all the good relationships in my life and practise gratitude for them, I continue to attract more positive relationships. There are still times when relationships in my life wane or dissolve, but I realise that they are no longer meant to be, and that is okay. I do not stay in the sadness of the loss for too long or allow it to feed any negative thoughts about being unworthy and unloved. Instead, I silently thank them for the value they added to my life while they were part of it and wish them the best for their lives. As long as I continue to love who I am, I genuinely think that I will always be in the company of amazing people. The flow-on effect is harnessing positivity and investing that energy into my relationships. Having great people in your life reflects how you feel about yourself.

I have recently turned 40 and often think about the day I lost my mother. It was the most challenging day I can remember, and it came with complex emotions and grief. But it was a wake-up call and showed me how holding onto the past and clinging to self-hatred and negativity were impacting my life. It sparked a 27-year self-love journey of self-discovery, acceptance, learning, and growing.

I am entering a new decade grateful for wonderful friends, a great partner, a job with great coworkers, and a fantastic relationship with my stepdad. My sister and I are closer than ever before. I also have loving support from my aunt and uncle. I understand that things change constantly, but these changes do not dictate who I am or my worth.

Most of all, I love myself enough to put myself first and not feel guilty. I make the most of every chance life gives me to achieve my objectives and dreams. I have a lot of love to give others as a result of doing this, but not at the expense of my wellbeing.

Important lessons learned from my experience for your journey towards self-love

1. Be kind to yourself and accept yourself and all your flaws; the world is full of harsh words and critics. You do not need to add your inner critic to that. Speak kindly to yourself, and don't call yourself mean things. Always take the time to celebrate how far you have come and how much you have grown. Do this each day, not just on your birthday.

2. Take responsibility and be accountable. Remember, this is your life. The timing will never be perfect for that next big

step in your life. You may believe your circumstances are not ideal, but that shouldn't hold you back from reaching to meet your goals and dreams. Instead, take responsibility for your life, and seize the moment. Take opportunities to read, learn from others and listen to yourself.

3. Be grateful for yourself, as well as everything and everyone in your life – including the adverse events, as these events are helping to move you onto something better. Try to notice at least one beautiful, small thing around you every single day. Make a note of it and be grateful for it.

4. Don't be afraid to let go of toxic people. You can still do this and be grateful. Understand that not everybody is on your journey and may not be ready to take responsibility for the energy they put out into the world. If someone is bringing negative vibes into your life, it might mean you need to step away from them. Don't be afraid to do this; whilst it may be painful in the short term, it will be liberating and vital in the long term. Remember to protect your vibe. It's not rude or wrong to remove yourself from situations or the company of people who are draining you.

5. It is a marathon, not a sprint; allow yourself to make mistakes. We're told from a young age, "nobody's perfect; everyone makes mistakes." As we get older, we feel like we cannot allow ourselves to fail. Cut yourself some slack! Make mistakes so you can learn and grow from them. You'll look back on these mistakes and see they were the stepping stones to being the best you.

Self-Love

If, right now, you don't feel worthy of love or self-love, think about how far you've come and how you've survived. You're here, right now, reading this for a reason. Practise gratitude and know that you are a powerful and unique being. Self-love may not happen overnight, but be kind and patient with yourself. With time, you'll see how self-love emanates from you.

CHAPTER 3

That Inner Voice

Brent Lindsay

"The journey to self-love starts with paying attention to that little voice in our heads. It's the voice that tells us to be kind to ourselves, to prioritise our needs, and to celebrate our accomplishments."

Have you ever heard that little voice in your head that tells you what to do or what not to do? That inner talk that guides your way, nudges your attention, and provides a positive direction for your life? If only we could listen quicker, get the message, and know what we need to fix. But sometimes, we do the best with what we have until we learn how to do better.

For me, that inner voice was first drowned out by the trauma I experienced as a child and teenager. I went through terrible experiences that created a negative, victim, lack, and unworthy self-image. And those negative emotional events created a pathway through life of feeling unloved, disenfranchised and cheated.

As a child, I was in a constant struggle at school due to my learning difficulties. I felt like I was always one step behind everyone else. It was like they understood what the teacher was saying, and I was always the one left confused and frustrated.

My school years were marred by bullying and abuse. I was often singled out by other kids for being different, and some of my teachers seemed to take pleasure in disciplining me. I'll never forget the primary school teacher who regularly locked me in a cupboard as punishment for my learning difficulties. It was a traumatic experience that I still carry with me to this day.

But, it wasn't just at school that I struggled. When I was young, I lost my father. It was a devastating blow to my young self, and I felt like I had lost a part of myself. I remember feeling lost, alone, and overwhelmed with grief, struggling to come to terms with the sudden and permanent loss of such an important figure in my life. Just a few years before, my grandfather had passed away as well, compounding my sense of loss and making me feel even more adrift in a world that felt increasingly uncertain and unfair.

My mother did her best to fill the void, but it was never the same, especially as she remarried shortly after and became a stepmother to two teenage children from my stepfather's previous marriage. This new family dynamic meant that my mother had to divide her attention across a lot of us and while I understood and accepted this, it was still difficult for me. There were times when I needed her, but she was spread thin looking after everyone and I felt like I was not a priority.

It was challenging to navigate my feelings of abandonment and rejection, and I often felt alone and unsupported. It was a tough adjustment for me, and I struggled to accept my new family situation.

While I tried to be open to the possibility of forming a connection with my stepfather, who I actually shared common interests with, he was unable at that point to embrace and cultivate that connection.

As a result, I never really had a male role model or mentor in my life, and this struggle to form close relationships with other men continued as I got older. I saw how my peers were able to form close bonds with their fathers, grandfathers, uncles, and other male figures, and I couldn't help but feel a sense of envy and longing.

In my teens I formed a friendship with a boy in my neighbourhood. We shared an adventurous spirit and eventually became more like brothers than friends. When you have good friends who truly care about you as he did, they can help you see your worth and value as a person and so this friendship (and the inner talk that followed) gave me a sense of belonging and acceptance that I had been lacking for years.

Unfortunately a few years after our friendship formed I witnessed my best friend drown in a terrible accident. I was unable to get to him and could only watch as it happened. I found myself constantly replaying the events of that day in my mind, wondering what I could have done differently, and wishing that somehow things could have turned out differently.

Losing him felt like a cruel joke. I couldn't understand why life was so unfair. Again I felt completely alone in my grief. It seemed like no one could truly understand the depth of my pain, or the sense of loss that I was experiencing.

These repeated experiences of trauma through my early years only served to reinforce my belief that life was unfair and I was powerless to change it. I began to internalise this narrative of victimhood, which led to ongoing feelings of shame, inadequacy, and hopelessness.

I constantly felt like an outsider, always on the fringes, and began seeking validation through risky and destructive behaviours through my later teens. I started to abuse drugs and alcohol, engaged in promiscuity, and acted in a deceitful and unreliable manner to cope with my anxiety and traumas. I could not look at myself in the mirror without feeling like I was not enough. I did not love myself. I felt like a victim of my circumstances, unable to break free from the cycle of pain and disappointment.

As I got older I began to seek love and acceptance in my relationships, but it always seemed to elude me. I would often find myself in codependent relationships with partners who cheated on me, which only added to my feelings of insecurity and low self-esteem.

For years, I ignored that inner voice guiding me out. I brushed it off as insignificant, something that was always there but never really mattered. I told myself lies to feel better, to justify my actions, and to hide from the truth. I convinced myself that I wasn't good enough, that I was unworthy of love and attention.

As a result, I was living a life of chaos and instability, always on the edge of disaster. I felt lost and alone.

Alicia Ann Wade

I first hit rock bottom when I was 23 years old.

Mixing with the wrong people and getting into the wrong situations I found myself living in a room in a drug dealer's house. I had hit my lowest point and didn't know what to do with my life.

But, that's when I heard the little voice in my head for the first time in years.

It was a faint whisper at first, but it grew stronger and clearer as time went on. It was my inner voice telling me that I was worth more than what I was putting myself through. It told me that I deserved to be happy and loved, but I needed to make a change in my life to achieve those things.

Thanks to my mother I was able to take action and get out of that situation and I slowly began to turn my life around. I started by taking care of myself physically, eating healthy, exercising, and quitting drugs and alcohol. I was trying to pick up the pieces of my life after years of a wild lifestyle.

It was during this time that I met my wife. We fell in love and tried to make steps forward in our lives together. But our relationship was built on a foundation of co-dependency and the wrong frame of mind as I was too weighed down by my traumas and only went into the marriage as I was desperate for someone to love me.

Ultimately, our values and expectations were vastly different, and our relationship became toxic. Despite this, I found myself agreeing to move across the country with her even though I didn't want to and I continued to stay in an unhappy marriage for too long.

Self-Love

I spent the next decade struggling with myself, ignoring the voice inside and stuck in a bad situation in order to stand by my children.

For years I struggled to balance work and family with my traumas and was constantly overwhelmed by my anxieties. I started my own business to make more money but the more I worked, the less time I had for my family, and when I worked for others, I experienced a cycle of abusive bosses and difficult workplaces.

I couldn't keep my business and finances afloat, my family was falling apart, and my own personal wellbeing was in shambles.

I was a mess, completely withdrawn, exhausted, negative in victim mode, there was a huge disconnect with my wife, and in my inner truth I was living a life so far away from my core self.

I teetered on the edge of worthlessness, self-loathing, failure, and suicide in hopes of finding peace and rest, as I was utterly exhausted and shattered. Rock bottom loomed close again.

I knew my marriage had ended, and the hardest thing I had to do was leave my kids. The weight of that decision to move out was compounded by having lost my own father at a young age. I couldn't bear the pain and anxiety they must have gone through, but I kept telling myself that they were better off with a dad who was alive and living away than a dead one.

But, the pain of missing my children and simultaneously going through the emotional turmoil of both bankruptcy and divorce took a heavy toll and to fill the void a series of bad relationships with women quickly followed in the years after. More relationship codependency, more toxicity, a continual lack of clarity in my purpose and an inability to sustain a positive mindset.

For the second time I found myself at rock bottom.

I still remember the day like it was yesterday. I had faced several challenges throughout my life, but this was truly the lowest point. The weight of all the traumas and struggles had finally caught up with me, and I felt completely lost and alone.

It was a difficult time, but deep inside I knew that something needed to change if I was ever going to find happiness and self-love. Even in my darkest moments, that inner voice persisted, whispering to me that there was a better way.

I was tired of feeling lost and alone, tired of living a life that was based on the opinions and expectations of others. I knew that I had to take control of my life and finally start listening to that inner voice that had been trying to guide me all along.

And so, I began my journey of self-love.

Thanks to the suggestion of connecting with a life coach I was able to take the first step to taking better care of my mental health.

As I embarked on my own journey into studying coaching, psychology, and human behaviour, I began to acquire the ability to release my victim mentality and started to embrace a life of self-acceptance and positive thinking. And most importantly, I learned to listen to that inner voice, to trust it, and to act on its guidance and to begin the difficult work of healing and self-love.

This transformation was a gradual process and did not occur overnight, but with consistent effort, I started to see improvements in my mindset and overall well-being.

As I began to work on cultivating self-love, I realised that one of the biggest barriers standing in my way were my limiting beliefs. These were the negative thoughts and beliefs that I had internalised about myself over the years, such as "I'm not good enough," "I don't deserve love," or "I'll never be successful." These beliefs had held me back for so long, keeping me trapped in a cycle of self-doubt and negativity.

However, by focusing on self-acceptance and challenging these beliefs, I was able to break free from their hold. I started to recognize when these thoughts would pop up and instead of automatically accepting them as true, I would question their validity. I would ask myself, "Is this really true? Is there evidence to support this belief, or is it just a story I'm telling myself?".

By doing this, I began to let go of my limiting beliefs and the negative emotions that had held me back for so long. I was no longer living in the past or being controlled by my fears and doubts. Instead, I was able to embrace the present moment and focus on creating a more positive and fulfilling life.

I learned to acknowledge and validate my own feelings, and to practise self-compassion when faced with challenging situations. By learning to love and accept myself for who I was, rather than constantly seeking validation from others, I was finally able to break free from the cycle of victimhood and create a more fulfilling and positive life.

Instead of feeling like a victim, I felt like a survivor. I had overcome so much, and I knew that I was strong enough to handle whatever came my way. I no longer saw myself as the helpless boy with learning difficulties, the young man who lost his father too soon, or the victim of bullying and abuse. I saw myself as a survivor who had come out the other side with more resilience and inner strength than ever before.

Learning to love and accept myself was not easy, and it took time and practice. But with each small step I took, I felt more empowered and less like a victim. I began to trust my own thoughts and feelings, and I acted on them rather than seeking validation from others.

I also learned the importance of practising self-care and setting boundaries. I made sure to take care of my physical and emotional needs, and I learned to say no to things that didn't serve me or that would harm me. I surrounded myself with people who lifted me up and supported me, rather than those who brought me down.

Forgiving myself for my mistakes and accepting my humanness was another crucial part of my journey towards self-love. I learned that making mistakes is a natural part of growth and that it doesn't diminish my worth as a person.

Living intentionally became a priority for me, and I set clear goals for myself that aligned with my values and purpose. As I accomplished these goals, I felt a deep sense of fulfilment and pride in myself.

By breaking free from the cycle of victimhood and cultivating self-love, I was able to create a more fulfilling and positive life for myself. I learned that I was worthy of love and respect, and that my happiness was in my own hands.

I started building new businesses, completing my MBA, and building new loving relationships. I reconnected with my children and started spending more time on the hobbies and experiences that gave me joy.

And now, through my coaching school, I share what I have learned with others so that they too can break free from victimhood and live a life of self-love and acceptance. I found a way to turn my pain into purpose.

Looking back on my life, I know that each challenge taught me a valuable lesson and helped me become the person I am today. I am grateful for every experience that has led me here to a life of joy, fulfilment, and purpose. I know that there will still be challenges and obstacles along the way, but I am confident that I can handle them. I am no longer a victim of my circumstances. I am the master of my destiny.

--

Words to guide...

The journey to self-love starts with paying attention to that little voice in our heads. It's the voice that tells us to be kind to ourselves, to prioritise our needs, and to celebrate our accomplishments. Yet, for many of us, that voice is drowned out by self-doubt, negative self-talk, and societal expectations. We find ourselves living a life that doesn't align with our true selves, feeling disconnected and unfulfilled. But the good news is that self-love is a skill that can be learned and cultivated, and it all begins with listening to that inner voice.

The road to self-love is not always a smooth one. For many of us, it's a journey filled with twists and turns, highs and lows, and moments of self-doubt and uncertainty. But at the core of this journey lies a simple truth: that inner voice, that guidance that steers the way, that nudge that gets your attention, is always there, waiting for you to listen and heed its message.

CHAPTER 4

Self-care is not Selfish

Kathryn Dawe

"I love that I get to love myself more. I love that I get love, and I love that I can now give love also."

"Self-care is not selfish". Tell that to a God-fearing, self-professed people-pleasing working mother of five…

The day I first heard this declaration, I felt resistance… or was it outright, sneering denial? Either way, I wasn't prepared or ready for the lesson I was about to learn. And what a journey it has been! Whoever said this declaration, was obviously not taught that one must "deny oneself and put others first" or "sacrifice oneself for others." They hadn't learned the same lessons I had, and clearly, they had it all wrong!

(Well, that's what use to think anyway.)

As a result, I spent most of my 40+ years living what "I thought" was the path to salvation. This is the life script I was raised on, the message instilled in me from a young age, the lessons of a child of service. So why was it that I felt shut down, hidden, repressed, and masked? Why did I feel so invisible? Why did I long to live a fantasy where I only dreamed about where I could be "me"? How was I to know that I was on a slippery path to self-denial, self-loathing, victim mindset, and shame for most of my growing life? If only someone had explained it differently to me… How often I have heard these words spoken to me… How often I have spoken them to myself… I guess it's only when we know something different that we can experience it.

"Share your whole story and whole heart," says Brene Brown.

This is my experience, the discovery journey I went on in resistance to believing in self-love.

Being born into an unhappy marriage, where the only memories I have of my parents as a couple are of them fighting, I quickly realised how miserable life is in general. Living in a small unit in a hotel, I often witnessed drunk men drowning their worries in self-pity and loathing (not that I understood that at the time). I was warned about 'staying away' from these people and grew up scared of most 'big people' I met. My mother worked hard cleaning rooms and working as a waitress, while my dad helped run the hotel in return for board and benefits. I felt so much of those young years, afraid… not just of those people outside my home walls, but also of the loud emotions that were heard from within, how could I know to self-regulate? No one was around to teach me. I remember from a very young age that I was able to 'dream' my way into an imaginary world where I got to choose the characters and settings of my alternate reality. I was able to imagine a place where people were happy and content, safe, and wanted. I later learned that this was the beginning of a coping strategy called 'dissociation', a mental process where a person disconnects from their thoughts, feelings, memories, or sense of identity. It was a way of experiencing what I wasn't getting in my world right then—somewhere I could feel safe in my mind, even if I didn't feel safe in my actual physical location. I wouldn't say I had "clinically" diagnosed dissociation; however, I know that I often daydreamed, and as I got older and more practised, I'd often find myself turning up to places on autopilot or sometimes listening to whole conversations without hearing a word. Some might say I was undisciplined or 'had my head in the clouds', but for me, it was my reality. I honestly don't know if it was because of that or because of my innocence, trustworthiness, and vulnerability, but I seemed to be a prime target for people looking to take advantage of me. It's like I had "vulnerable" tattooed on my forehead; perhaps I was naive. In any case, I had a poor sense of trust that led me into situations where children shouldn't have been.

Now I'm not sharing these things lightly here… it's taken me decades of counselling and coaching to be able to write about these things… You see, for so long I just figured there was something 'wrong' with me, and as a result, I needed 'fixing'… So, when things went wrong (as they often did), I convinced myself that it was my fault and that if I had been a 'good girl', this would not have happened. The internal verbal self-talk in my head reminded me time and time again about how damaged I was. It's interesting to reflect on this now, realising the stories we tell ourselves as children… the learned behaviours we bring to our adult lives, oblivious to the reality that children are often victims, the innocent ones we need to protect ... Simply put, we had no idea how to defend ourselves.

So, where were my parents during this later time, you may ask? Well, my father left when I was 7, to enjoy life with a younger version 10 years his junior, and my mother spent the next two decades 'looking for love'... Her pursuit of this meant many more unhealthy relationships for not just her but also for me and my sister along the way. I wish I had cultured the learnings in this book earlier to share with my mother the secrets I've learned about love now... (sneak peek... it results from internal work!) Unfortunately, my mother has Alzheimer's at the time I'm writing this and spends most of her days unaware of her deeper relationships.

My mother's search for love drew her to Christianity, and she sought love in Christ. This seemed to have some comfort for her, but it came with lots of other complications. For one, the Christian belief of some was that women were 'less' than men and, as such, they 'needed' a male in their lives to fulfil them. In desperation (I believe) my mother settled for someone who 'seemed' knowledgeable in scriptures and who (she thought) would provide the needed male presence in our small family... I don't quite know what crazy thoughts played out in her mind... but, I ended up with a step-father at age 12... that was one of the tragic parts of my life... a time when children start to stretch their independence, I was suddenly thrown into a world where I was "strongly encouraged" to call this man my 'dad' and introduced to physical discipline, not the discipline of discipleship like a teacher to instruct, but the discipline of leather belts with brass buckles on bare legs... It's no wonder the self-talk I adopted at this time of my life told me I was worthless and deserving of punishment... I remember one distinct moment that was very influential in my teen years, it was soon after the marriage and I had done something "wrong" again... maybe worn a skirt too high, or taken too long coming home... maybe I'd back-chatted... I can't remember, but I do remember the consequences... "go to your room, and wait there until I come... think about what you have done and I'll come and deal with you when I'm ready" ... I received the belt... cried a bit and felt sorry for myself, but what was different this time was I could hear my mother crying in the room next door... I hadn't realised until now how this was impacting her, so I went to her room and knocked on the door... when prompted I whispered "I'm okay mum, I've stopped crying" ... How was I to know that this would anger my stepfather? How was I to know that he would respond the way he did? How did I know that the lesson I learned that day would still haunt me long into my adult life? ... he marched me straight back to my room and dealt me the harshest beating I had received... It was at this time I realised that it was better to shut up and stay down... It was a harsh lesson to learn for a young teenage child... Although I now know that, how did I know then? Who was going to show me love? ... How could I expect to even start to understand what "self-love" was? It wasn't until decades later that I found out that my mother had also received the lashings of my step father's anger, domestic violence wasn't talked about in my church... We wanted to avoid looking flawed. Now, I'm not telling you about this experience to win your sympathy or to put you on edge. I'm also not telling you about it to incite your wrath. I'm telling you this to illustrate how childhood trauma or neglect can affect how we view the world for the rest of our lives. You have my permission to spread this to others.

Children are the innocent victims of 'big people's neglect.

I learned to be "the good Christian girl," doing well in school but having no value in education because "girls don't go to university," they said, and so as the years went on I "lost myself" I met my husband, got pregnant, had a beautiful, bouncy boy, and felt miserable. We lost our daughter at full term and only 3 days old. It's difficult to say whether my saddness was due to postpartum depression or simply because life wasn't as fulfilling as I had hoped (my expectations and reality didn't quite match). Regardless, it led to my second pregnancy (after a few miscarriages). This is what I had waited for; I finally felt like I was getting what I deserved—punishment for my selfishness and for the "bad" and "wrong" woman I had turned out to be. Even though I think this is one of my lowest points, it was during this period that I began to open up to journaling and writing down my emotions. I'm glad I did that now because I can reflect on what I was thinking and feeling at the time. In addition to being a sacred period, it was also a period of significant personal development for me. After losing our daughter, I decided to pursue something for myself… I decided to study to become a teacher. Most of the members of my church probably believed that it was merely a coping mechanism for the loss and that I would eventually give up, but I was more determined than ever. I now had a purpose. I was going to be helping people. During this time, I went on to have 4 more healthy children (although the last one was a bit of a dramatic birth, having had placenta previa and accreta, which led to me delivering at the state royal hospital some 600km from home, followed by a full hysterectomy—a dramatic entry for our last child!).

Self-Love

I became a teacher, and I worked hard to balance life between work, home duties, parenting, etc., but it wasn't long before I became numb and emotionless again, doing the "doing" but not "living". I had become a self-abandoned, overweight complainer. I no longer found joy in the small things, and I even found it hard to find passion in my greatest love—horses.

It was then that I met a confidence coach, Bianca, who gave me the facts! I had stopped feeling. I was shut down and empty.

So, what did I do with this new information? Denied it, of course! Well, that day was the first day I had a full-blown panic attack… the type where you can't breathe, you think that something is going to eat you, and you are paralysed. On reflection, it's such a strange feeling, it makes no sense whatsoever, and yet you have no way to stop it… It's like your dreams and nightmares all intermingle into your reality, and you don't know what to believe anymore. In that moment, my heart beat a hundred miles an hour, the sweat on my forehead tripled, my palms became sweaty, and I squeaked my reply through my reddened face! "I'm fine! I'll survive" … One of the most terrifying experiences I've ever had was a panic attack. I was left with no choice but to sit in a ball and rock until the noises in my head subsided.

I knew I needed more than the self-help books I had been delving into to find answers. I began looking for a counsellor.

This was the beginning of years of personal development and soul-searching in order to "find myself". I connected with a clinical psychologist who listened and validated my feelings. At first, I wanted her to fix me, but I soon learned that it wasn't about 'fixing', it was about 'healing'. I joined self-help groups, and I read a lot of books. I gained more knowledge about concepts like C-PTSD, abuse, relationship trauma, dissociation, HSP, and others. All of which gave my understanding of my university studies and my personal experiences a great deal more clarity. I finally started to feel the veil over my eyes open and my heart begin to expand. I started to see and feel things differently. I started to understand that in order to feel love, it starts from the inside.

I'm curious if you can identify with any of this. This marked the beginning of my journey towards self-discovery and development for me. I've finally come to the realisation that "me" is the most important person in my life, and that I must put "me" first in order to preserve my life. This was a very foreign concept to me; once I felt I had no voice, I now see it as my freedom and power to own my life and make choices that would protect me and make me stronger. As a result, I now feel more free, more alive, and more fulfilled. I don't need to "day-dream" any longer to escape my reality; I get to live in the present now, appreciating the small things along with the bigger things. I get to spend more quality time with my family and can now teach our children the lessons I've learned. It's not all rosy; there are down moments, but I get to experience these on a whole new level with compassion, patience, and kindness.

I adore being able to love myself more. I appreciate the love I receive as well as the ability to reciprocate. As part of this, I'm learning more about myself, the things I love and value, the people I can trust, and the beliefs I no longer hold on to. I know more about "who I am" and how to set healthy boundaries—all signs of a healthy version of "self-love".

If this story resonates with you and you'd like to know more about self-love and finding yourself, feel free to contact me through my website https://kathryntd99.wixsite.com/kady.

Want a free copy of "20 tips to self-love" booklet – follow this link… https://kathryntd99.wixsite.com/kady/contact-4

"Self-love is not selfish" … sending love and light to guide your way.

"You yourself, as much as anybody in the entire universe, deserve your love and affection" – Buddha

CHAPTER 5

The 9R Process Mindset

Kate Taylor

"Self-love starts with working on healing the inside from our hurt and emotional pain."

My journey towards self-love has spanned my entire life. This is what I mean when I say that people are challenging me for who I am: I've been repeatedly bullied, and I've had people try to control my thoughts. I have always had an independent mind and would occasionally be outspoken, whether it was in the workplace, among friends, in interpersonal and romantic relationships, or among family members, to portray more accurately who I am. I was the little, frail, quiet girl with a small voice. Once she stuck up for herself, I would get a telling-off and be brought back to where they wanted me. But hey, if others can do it, why can't I set my boundaries and advocate for myself? It would appear that I was not permitted to do this and that I had to be subject to their control. I became the person I am today as a result of this behaviour because I was motivated to learn how to be the best person I could be. I had a serious illness during my twenties that thankfully, I overcame. I was given a clinical depression and anxiety diagnosis after my father passed away. Extreme panic attacks would happen to me. Once I was healthy, I then relocated to Australia. I understood that I wasn't deserving of being treated that way and that I was capable of more if I permitted myself to be who I truly am. After experiencing an emotionally abusive relationship, grieving the loss of my mother, and building my brand, I decided to work on my self-worth, increase my level of self-love, and establish my credibility. I have lived through the emotional pain and found ways to love myself more than ever. During this time, I wrote my first book "Leading to a New You". The 9-R Process Mindset Method was developed.

A technique to use repeatedly is the 9 R Process Mindset. Self-love is a journey that is constantly changing. There are ups and downs for us. Building on our self-love as we grow through the stages, each time we are levelling up, and when we go through each stage, we then make another break, and the cycle starts all over again. We never stop growing and developing as lifelong learners. If you are into being the best you can be, let's begin from the beginning with the 9-R Process Mindset Method.

This is a system that involves the 9 R's: reframe, reset, re-adjust, restart, refocus, review, result, rinse, and repeat.

All these parts make up a process of self-love. We need to do the work and take the steps to learn how to love ourselves from our heart space. This is the love that will be there through thick and thin. Sometimes, it won't feel like that, but we can go to that heart space and know that it will be there waiting for us to grasp it and hold on to it, even when we're going through a rough patch. Once you have enabled the self-love switch to be on, it will always be on because you have permitted yourself to love yourself within your heart space. No one can take this away from you. It is yours to keep. Let's go through each part and see how they can assist us in our growth moving forwards. Let's start with the first one: reframe.

1: REFRAME

Reframing is changing your internal language and the language you are speaking to others. We do this by changing our negative words into positive ones. When we do this, our internal world changes. We need to create a new habit; it takes 30 days to embed a new habit, according to Atomic Habits, written by James Clear. This is a good idea to join other like-minded people to help you stay on track and accountable.

2: RESET

Reset is the next one that we will go through. This is about resetting your thinking—resetting your mind, body, and soul into alignment with all that is. It starts with your environment, your internal world, and your inner core of being. We do this by starting to use your words in a way that will serve you in the best possible way. It all starts with yourself talking by embodying and feeling what you're saying to yourself with the fullest intention. We do this by not allowing the negative energy to overtake our mind; once that happens, you feel it throughout your body, and this can make you start to feel unwell. We then need to reset the way we think and feel those positive

Self-Love

feelings in our bodies. There are steps to help get you started, which will be explained in my book "Leading into a New You". The first step is to

1. Get back into a routine
2. Stay away from social media and mass media.
3. Let your alone time work for you.
4. Meditate or practise mindfulness
5. Exercise more.
6. Read more fiction.
7. Write it out.
8. Listen to music.
9. Get more sleep.
10. Ask for help.

Then we need to readjust the mind and body.

3. READJUST

Your beliefs become your thoughts. Your thoughts become your actions. Your actions control your success, and your happiness creates your present.

Readjusting means accepting that your thoughts need changing. Our mental sets are formed through prior experiences and emotions. Once we are aware, we can flip the switch and focus on changing our mindset. We need to adjust our thinking; our thinking can change the way our body feels and how we cope with different situations. It is not just an internal process; our internal thinking can alter our physical state. There are steps to changing your mindset in the adjusting phase; this phase will come and go as we move up the levels of being our best selves.

When we accept that our thinking needs changing if we're experiencing inner negativity because our minds are formed through prior experiences and emotions, once we are aware, we can flip the switch and focus on changing our mindset. Adjusting our thinking can change the way our body feels and how we cope with different situations. That is why we are adjusting to all that our mindset is changing inside us. It is not just internal processes; our internal thinking can alter our physical state. This is why I call it "adjusting," and self-care is important. There are steps to changing your mindset in the adjusting phase; this phase will come and go as we move up levels of being our best selves.

4. RESTART

Start each day with gratitude. Wake up each morning with gratitude for a new day. Have gratitude for even the smallest of things if you are going through a rough time. This will help to make you stronger internally; you may not notice it to start with, but you will over time. When you start out being positive, you are setting yourself up for success.

5. REFOCUS

What do I mean by "refocus"? If you're disconnected from your end goal, by re-focusing on the result with a vision and mission in place, you will gain greater motivation to continue what you set out to achieve. You would already know what it would feel like once you had completed the desired goal. Those feelings may include happiness, joy, excitement, pride, a sense of achievement, and success.

What are your top priorities? Organise them in the order that they get done. What are the three objectives that you are trying to achieve each day?

There are many ways that you can regain your focus to bring you back to being grounded, such as breath work, which brings the oxygen back through your body and up to your brain. It calms you down when you take notice of your breathing. Allow yourself to relax and stay in mindfulness, in the present moment, without letting your mind wander and overthink things that are not helping with your end goal in sight.

6: REVIEW

Review how you are thinking, and review your life changes; what I mean by this is that have you noticed any differences? How are you feeling? How are other people responding to you? Have you noticed that maybe you are happier and things that you used to react to that once hindered your progress are no longer a problem? People start to see changes in you and react in different ways because they don't understand that you are evolving into a new you. When we take this journey of saying yes to ourselves and living a fuller life, people either come with us on our journey and want to learn more, or they start to drop off because they don't understand the new you. That is okay; it can be sad and hard to lose people that you were once close to, but you will get to meet up with the ones who can better support you along your path.

7. RESULTS

What results are you seeing? Have you accomplished anything? Have you reached your outcomes and benchmarks? Are they what you wanted? Did you celebrate your achievements and acknowledge yourself for your efforts in pushing through your comfort zones? If not, why not? Go deeper into why you haven't reached them and ask for help to figure it out, put it in a structured system, and add accountability.

8. RINSE

So, we nearly finished the 9 R Process Mindset Method, and it is time to rinse it all out, shake it off, and take a break. Just like the washing machine, squish out all the unwanted dirty water. This is a process to remember; changes do not happen overnight. It took me years to move through hard mental blocks and fears from living in other people's dreams and expectations. Being emotionally abused by people who say that we are not good enough, we need to rinse out where we have come from, look at how far we have come, keep our heads held high, and see, hear, and feel where we are heading. Our past doesn't exist, and neither does our future. Be your best self in the now.

9. REPEAT

For us to improve and get better at who we are becoming and to grow and expand in our self-worth, we need to repeat the process or change it to suit the new you. Each time we learn, we grow forwards, we become stronger within ourselves, and our fear changes. We want to start being seen and not afraid of showing up or saying what we feel because we believe in ourselves more, we know our self-worth and we love ourselves more. We show greater value to the world. It is okay to repeat a process in this regard, this is not like being in school, and this has nothing to do with school. This is about you. Your inner light, your little tinker bell inside you with all the magic and that little tinker bell has a wand, it is up to you when you start to wave it around like you don't care, use it to your advantage. Let Tinkerbell come out of you and shine, spread your love to others and they will then light up. Once we start to expand our newfound love and self-worth for ourselves we start to attract the people who are drawn to us, they see you in a different light, they either want to get to know you more and follow you on your journey and support you, or they will move on because they don't know the new you if they are not a moth trying to dip your light. That can be hard to deal with, but you will find new people on your level who will notice you, and provide you with fresh, greater opportunities.

Self-love starts with working on healing the inside from our hurt and emotional pain. Take the first step by permitting yourself to love yourself. Live and lead a life that you love.

CHAPTER 6

The Hero Within & The Hero Without

Josh Solomon

"Personal development can be scary. Sometimes, it can feel like walking down a dark tunnel with your hands out in front of you, hoping you don't run into something."

To my two boys Elijah and Zavier,

You gave me hope in a time where I had none. I can never express how grateful I am to be your father. Your love humbles me every day and in the space of your greatness I feel inspired to live at my highest vibration, to always be in integrity, and stay true to myself. You are my reasons why...

There are many places I could inject you to get a sense of the hero's journey that I've been privileged to participate in. Like so many of you, my life was an uphill battle, not only vertical, but also inside out and upside down. Like every good story there are usually a handful of moments that define it. I want to share mine with you to highlight the actuality of the rollercoaster that life can be when we don't realise that at any time, we can choose to hop off and stand on steady ground.

The Hero's Journey

I was 3 weeks into my deployment to Afghanistan. What a time in my life that was. To be in such a tight knit group of people all sharing a common goal, fighting for the freedom and safety and others and willing to lay down your life for the man or woman standing next to you is a feeling that will stay with me through this life and the next.

Life over in Tarin Kowt was, to say the least, an eye opener to the world outside of our own. For those of us who are lucky enough to live in a developed country, we are just that… Lucky.

One of the things that stays with me the most from my time in Afghanistan, for very contrasting reasons, is the degradation of the human condition. Seeing the conditions that the local people lived in broke my heart every time we went out on patrol yet at the same time, they were able to remain so happy and content with their lives.

Children coming up to our vehicles on patrol was a common fixture. Seeing how excited they were for us to give the fresh water, cans of soft drink, chocolates, pens, and paper still lights me up to this day. On the occasions it was warranted, my crew commander and I would play music for them and watch these kids in these war-torn areas start to dance around and just be so amazingly in the moment. It's like they had completely forgot that at any time insurgent forces could start raining down gunfire or launch clandestine rockets into their compounds and villages.

And then, on other occasions we would patrol through the same area and the scene was completely different. We could feel the tension in the air. Locals hiding for fear of retaliation by the insurgents' forces if they were seen to be talking with or even anywhere near us.

To this day one of the memories that haunts me the most was seeing a young boy, maybe as young as my oldest son was at the time of this writing, being beaten with a rope with a knot tied in the end of it. I could hear the pain in the screams of the young boy. But what sticks with me the most is the fear in the eyes of who I presumed to be the father of that boy. Imagine being in so much fear for your village and family that beating a child with a rope for doing nothing more than curiously investigating a patrol of Soldiers moving through their village, that lashing out in such a physical way was the best option for the safety of your family.

I later found out that it was common practice for fathers of young families as a way to show the insurgent forces hiding out in their villages that they were loyal to the Taliban and not supporting foreign militaries.

Imagine just for a moment how much fear they must be in…

But of all the things I experienced over there from the highs of the comradery with my brothers in arms to the despair of the local people, it was something that happened back home that lead me

Self-Love

to the depths of my deepest darkest cave. I had my trust broken by someone I loved.

On deployment it's the thoughts of back home that keep us going. Those long sleepless nights not knowing if at any time a stray rocket would wake us up or take us out permanently, the long days patrolling constantly scanning and wondering if that pile of rubbish is actually a pile of rubbish or whether or not I would drive over and Improvised Explosive Device (IED) or even worse, not drive over it and have the vehicles behind me blow up and cost the lives of my fellow soldiers.

So, when I found out what happened back home, the thoughts that kept me going not only vanished, but they too were also fighting against me. I had never felt so betrayed in my life. With nowhere to turn I was left to battle the innermost thoughts without a shield, and it pains me to say that they got the best of me. I can remember sitting in the back of my Bushmaster Patrol Vehicle after a patrol one day cleaning my weapons, lost in the chaos of my fractured mind and staring at my pistol when someone walked around to the back of my vehicle, looked in and asked if I was ok. I remember it vividly because that was the first time I had ever thought about ending my own life with something in my hand that could do the job.

"It would be so easy" was the thought that was interrupted.

After weeks of trying to keep my shit together and still be an effective soldier I eventually lost the battle. I could feel the tension rising from the pit of my stomach, I was heading for a breakdown. One night back on MNBTK (Multinational Base Tarin Kowt) I told my bunkmate that I was going for a walk. I left my body armor in my room, strapped my pistol to my hip and started walking towards the Conex's at the back of the perimeter wall.

There I sat, in the midst of collapse. Betrayed by the person I loved and betrayed by my own mind. Lost in the chaos of negative thought loop after negative thought loop. There was only one way out... I still remember the feeling of my pistol pressed to my temple. The steel felt cool on my head against the heat of a dry Afghan night, the familiar clicking sound as I switched the safety off and the frightening feeling of my finger resting on the trigger. I don't remember if I was screaming in my head or out loud, but the sound was deafening.

Like so many of you, I know what it's like to be so far down in your cave that it feels like checking out is the only way out. I know what it feels like to be strapped into the roller coaster screaming to be let off. That kind of experience changes you.

It took me 6 years and a whole heap of bad decisions to overcome that experience. But I'm here standing before you in the most positive and empowering place I've ever been in. I've battled with the chaos of my mind. The voice of self-doubt, the feeling of unworthiness, the yo-yo of feeling great & motivated, then falling back into procrastination, overthinking and all other forms of self-sabotage

6 years of beating myself up, judging myself, comparing myself to others and constantly living in those 'why does this always happen to me', or 'I just can't ever seem to get it right' experiences. 6 years stuck on that same roller coaster from that ONE experience with

nothing but a bunch of drugs (prescription and non-prescription), and some guilt money that I didn't feel like I had earned, desperately searching for something outside of me to either numb the pain or distract me from the life I was constantly trying to escape.

The Shift

There comes a time in the hero's journey, usually when he or she is at their lowest. Laying in a rainy alleyway slumped up against a bin, or alone in a dark & creaky house with nothing but a head full of shitty memories.

Well, mine was a little different…

See, in those 6 years of personal hell, had you asked anyone how I was doing, or who I was, they would tell you a different story. They might say things like Josh is so outgoing. He's always the life of the party. Always a good time when Josh is here. Josh cares about people and really has his shit together considering what he's been through.

One thing I had learned to be good at during my time in the military was keeping my shit on the inside and putting on a solid "Alpha Male" front.

I had surrounded myself with the kind of people that look up to and leeched off Alpha male energy. I had the "perfect life" to them.

Status – Money – Power

I was in my early 30's, medically retired from the military, getting paid hundreds of thousands of dollars on a semi-regular basis, all of the time and all of the money with no need to work or do anything for it.

I had my 2 young boys on a week on week off co-parenting schedule with my ex-wife. My life was in perfect balance. One week it was dad-life. School runs, hanging out with my boys, spending every waking moment with them watching them and guiding them as they grew.

And the next week party life. Four & Five day benders snorting lines of cocaine off new women every weekend. Shouting all of my friend trips to various places, staying in high end hotels and getting all kinds of wasted, then drowning out the comedown with a handful of prescription pills.

My life was a rinse and repeat 2 week cycle based off a persona that I had created to protect myself from all of the bullshit I had been running from for so long now. To avoid my most feared truth…

That I was insignificant…

See this thing is, it was easier to be someone else than to face the horror that was my own self-image. When it comes to defense mechanisms, mine was the greatest in human history. I became so amazingly good at being whoever "they" wanted me to be to stop me from realizing that I had no idea who the hell I was. This went on for so long that at times, I forgot what I was running from. I would settle in just enough to get a glimpse of peace and happiness.

But that voice of depression never stays away for long…

Self-Love

The thing is, when your way of dealing with your problems is to run from them, you had better keep running. Because the moment you stop to smell the roses, those problems will catch up with you. And they always seem to pick up a couple more along the way…

This crazy lifestyle of mine went on for years. It wasn't all doom and gloom though. That life took me all over the world. I saw some of the most amazing sights. The Digital Art Museums and the Fushimi Inari shrine in Japan, The Majestic Fjords of Norway, a fun couple of days in Amsterdam and even a week-long holiday romance on the island of Majorca off the coast of Spain.

In fact even to this day I don't regret a single moment from that chapter of my life. Amongst the horde that were just in it for the free party, I met some of the most amazing people I've ever had the privilege of connecting with. Strengthened the bonds of some of my fellow soldiers, found my best friend in the whole world. Hell, I even found love again and had the most amazing 2 year relationship. Jen, Kat, Lance & Kit if you ever read this know that I wouldn't be the man I am today, the father I am today and living a life of true purpose and service that I am today if it wasn't for the love, respect and acceptance you showed my during those times

You all saw something in me that I didn't see myself. Some worthy of love. If it hadn't been for the genuine love that you showed to me time and time again when I was at both my best and my worst, I would never have even started down the pathway of personal discovery.

That's where it all turned around for me… Seeing people that I cared about more than my own life, flourish and grow around me. Seeing that I had a positive effect on the world beyond what I can throw money at and beyond the cool calm and collected persona I felt I had to put on.

They saw me in the depths of my cave and still they stayed. They saw me crying and they still stayed. They surprised me on my birthday, comforted me when I was feeling blue, defended me when others tried to gossip, protected me from the people who were only in it for money.

I didn't have to pretend anymore. I was home.

I often head that all good things must come to an end. I no longer agree with that statement. Because the very act of closing one door opens another. When you think about it, life is just a series of doors opening and closing. Each new door you walk through is there to teach you something. And you'll either learn the lesson that is there for you or you'll walk through the same door again and again until you do.

For me this repeated for years and years. Until one day, I had a realization. Doors open both ways… I had spent most of my adult life opening doors outwards in a constant search for my needs and desires to be met, when the only door I had ever needed to open was the door that opened in.

This single moment changed the trajectory of my life. It was time to figure out what I was truly capable of.

To everyone who played a role in my life up until this point, I am forever grateful for you.

The Game Changers

There's 2 frameworks that I would like to share with you that I feel have had the most phenomenal effects on my own life and the life of my clients. Sigmund Freuds 6 Core Needs of the Human Condition, and the power of gratitude.

To figure out who I was I needed to know a bit more about what the hell is this thing we call life. After fishing around in some beginners' ponds in the personal development realm (habits, nutrition, changing your environment) with moderate success, I began to recognise the patterns and behaviors and actions of others, as well as within my own thoughts and emotions.

This got me curious…. I was the common denominator in every single experience I had ever been through, yet had no idea how I operated. Enter Dr Joe Dispenza and a 12 month rabbit hole of neuroscience, epigenetics and spirituality, so I could fully understand and grasp the power of ***gratitude***.

From the first time I heard about *gratitude* I was hooked. I knew I had found the missing piece of the puzzle. Everything up until this point was all about the why. Gratitude gave me the how.

See, the thing about gratitude is that it carries one of the most powerful neuro-chemical signatures that we can create naturally.

When we are in states of gratitude, we are producing a juicy cocktail of neurochemicals that I like to call the **BIG 5**:

Serotonin – Mood stabilizer.
Endorphins – Natural pain reliever.
Oxytocin – Bonding or love chemical.
Nitric oxide – Vasodilator (increases blood flow).
Dopamine – Reward chemical.

And the wonderful thing about this is we can turn this on by thought alone. I want you to try it with me now. Close your eyes and take yourself back to a time where you were so amazingly grateful. Maybe someone did something for you or maybe you did something for yourself.

How good does it feel? Pretty amazing right?

Well with practice, you can use this to go back through the rolodex of your memories and change the association between the moment that has happened in your past, and the emotional (or neurochemical) reaction that you experience in the present day.

Imagine being able to take all of those negative emotions from your past that cloud your judgment of the present, and turn them into a library of amazing moments that you could use to create your future?

It's how I went from broken veteran on the verge of suicide, constantly running from my problems and relying on other people to fulfill my needs and desires, to having a thriving coaching business in under 2 years. It's the very first thing I teach my clients and the transformations that happen in their lives as a direct result of consciously becoming more grateful in their daily lives are indescribable.

It was Dr Joe Dispenza who said "We live in an age where it's not enough to know, we have to know how".

The most powerful *how* is the human condition. Learn how you operate, then operate yourself in any way that you want to achieve any outcome you desire.

I said this at the start, and I'll say it again. *Personal development can be scary. Sometimes it can feel like walking down a dark tunnel with your hands out in front of you hoping you don't run into something.*

The tools & frameworks you pick up along the way are like shining a light down the tunnel. Gratitude is that same light, but it shines from within you. It doesn't matter what happens or where you go. If you look for gratitude in every experience you're going to find it.

And when you do, get ready. Not only will you feel the effects of the **BIG 5,** you're very reality will get an upgrade and life will go from something you want to escape, to something you can't wait to experience.

The next game changer in your personal development journey is to know what your needs are

There are 6 fundamental needs of the human condition. These needs are:

1. Safety & Comfort (certainty)

2. Variety & Change
3. Significance
4. Love & Connection
5. Contribution
6. Growth

Needs 1-4 are the needs of desires of "what can I get". They belong to the personality. Needs 5 & 6 are the needs of the spirit. "What can I give & how can I grow".

These 6 needs are the drivers for everything we do in life. They sit behind every choice, every decision and every defining moment that you and I have ever been through in the past, present and into the future.

These needs are the reason we run self-sabotage patterns like procrastination, or even stay in jobs or relationships that we know aren't serving us. *Have you ever had something, that you know by doing it, will completely change your life?*

Maybe it's standing up to your boss, leaving that unfulfilling relationship, completing your studies, making a financial investment in yourself. Yet for some reason you just can't seem to get yourself to do it. You know exactly what you need to do (and probably how to do it) but you bail out or sabotage yourself every time... Sound familiar?

You know exactly what you need to do (and probably how to do it) but you bail out or sabotage yourself every time.

Let's add the framework of the 6 needs into the mix. The reason you probably not doing it is because even as shitty as some of those experiences are, you can predict what will happen if you don't take action. If it's predictable, it's safe, if it's safe it's comfortable. Even if it's shitty or abusive, you can predict the mechanisms of the experience therefore you know how to navigate them.

In fact, you can probably do this so well that you don't even need to think about it. The situation is triggered, and you switch to autopilot mode. Have the same conversations, the same dinners, the same life even if it's with different people.

What need do you feel is the strongest in these types of situations?

Safety & Comfort

Let's try one more so you can really feel the validity of this framework.

You've always been the kind of person that puts other people first. You say yes because that is what good people do. Even the times that you want to say no, you always end up saying yes. 20 mins later you're driving in your car thinking to yourself "why did I say yes to that?"

You can always be counted on to help someone and are known in your circles as the nice guy, or helpful girl. You struggle to voice your opinions because maybe you don't want to rock the boat. Saying things like "it's okay, what do you want to do?". Not necessarily a push over but your needs and desires always too be the last ones met and always quick to forgive or make excuses for others because you would rather be with people than to be alone...

Which is the need that you are fulfilling within this example?

Love & Connection

I want you to take a moment to consider these 6 needs and ask yourself this question. Where are they showing up in my life and what needs am I unconsciously not taking responsibility for by offloading them to the people and circumstances in my life?

You see, the most powerful being in the world is one who needs nothing. How can you begin the process of fulfilling your own needs? By realizing the there's no one coming to rescue you. No matter who you are, what you're doing or what stage of life you are in.

Because here is the kicker… No-one *can* rescue you. Even if they wanted to they couldn't. I've been on both sides of that coin. The rescuer and the person wanting to be rescued. Both roles are an unconscious form of self-abandonment. Both of these roles are you offloading the responsibility of you need to the people and things around.

These 6 fundamental needs of the human condition govern everything you do. They are the drivers for life, the motives for your actions, the inspiration for your desires, the operating manual for how you operate. Taking some time to explore them and understand how & where they are showing up, and how to fulfill them within yourself, is the key to understanding this roller coaster we call life. Sprinkle a little bit of gratitude into the mix and you've got the yourself the blueprint to a happy and fulfilling life.

Self-Love

Because the way out is not the way out. It's the way in. It was the doorway in that took me from broken veteran to Coach, Facilitator and Motivational Speaker, reconnected me with the love of my 2 boys, and saved my life. Because if you are not the hero within, you are the hero without...

Josh Solomon

CHAPTER 7

THE YES-A-HOLIC - Questioning everything

Nicole Pirrie

"Self-love is walking out the door with a twinkle in your eye, bringing ALL-OF-YOU-NESS, proclaiming 'I'm worth it, baby'...."

Have you ever had a full-blown argument with yourself? Like you vs. you inside your mind? I have had fairly diplomatic mental battles from time to time whether I should eat chocolate or not and of course we know who always wins that one. I generally fob opposing thoughts off and move on. But this particular day when I drove myself to hospital, my inner self was so pissed off. So annoyed and argumentative, which is normally not like me. Inside of me was having a shouting disagreement like 'you knew you didn't want to do this, so why did you do it' and retorted with 'it's the right thing to do by everyone else, so just shut up and get on with it.' I became even more conscious in the last part of this verbal wrestle. All sorts were being said but finally a defeated voice came out with; 'You didn't stand by YOUR beliefs, you didn't stand by YOUR values…

Self-Love

you just forgot about us'. I'm processing all these words like an old computer system struggling to upload a new program. Who is 'us' I asked myself. Were these voices 'parts' of me... yelling to be heard?

My poor heart feels hurt in more ways than one. Why did it take me this long to finally listen to my-self?

I've been a personal development junkie since I was a teenager and for the most part, I was seeking out ways to live my life so that my eighty-year old self doesn't clip me around the ears for not living life to the fullest. I'm all about self-help and in most cases 'shelf-help' because my vintage bookcase looks like a colourful village of motivation and positivity. I've kept a journal since I was young, picking it up to do those journal type things, occasionally moan and bitch about society or people in my life so I didn't have to voice it out loud.

It became my quest at a young age to be a good human, be kind, be positive, be easy-going, be respectful, keep a lid on strong opinions... and so on. You get the picture; I was trying to be a mixture of the Dalai Lama and Oprah basically. I was a ratbag of a child who once put press pins in my teacher's chair, so I really felt I had to turn my life around and strive for goodness.

I realise now there was a category of my self development journey that was missing all these years. That was self-love. I don't recall ever investing much time or energy into self-love, nor delving into what it means to 100% love myself enough to give less fucks about what others think. Not to mention, I couldn't bear to let people down. I have a sense of loving myself in the physical realm, but love at a core level to look after my well-being and respect for my boundaries has been very diluted countless times. Later in this chapter I delve deeply into what self-love looks like for a recovering yes-a-holic... I'll share my journey with coming to terms with one simple word. One word that has turned everything around.

I'm actually getting so excited to tell you this word as I write because had I been comfortable with this word for most of my people-pleasing life, I would have prevented break downs, burn out, anxiety and illness. That word my friends... is the glorious, simple word, NO.

Let me talk briefly about those values and beliefs, you know, the ones that my-self told me I had forgotten about? Values are the principles that are important to us. Whether we know them or not, we are living them. For example, if you go to the gym and eat healthy, I'd say you value health. Conversely, if you eat takeaway and watch tv all day, you probably value comfort and ease. What you value brings results.

Beliefs on the other hand are facts that you accept to be true, often without question.

They're formed throughout life and influenced by the way we were raised, where we lived, schooling, work environment, defining events and so much more. An example of a belief that old me held onto tightly was 'If I work really hard, say yes (to everyone) and be easy-breezy-happy-go-lucky... then I'm a good person'.

If we were to recognise and adhere to our own values and beliefs, we would be living 'in alignment'. We would have healthy and respectful boundaries, like a whole body 'hell YES' feeling about life. It's total self-love in action because these core guides keep us staying true to what we stand for and where we are heading. How many of us actually live them? How many of us would prefer to be liked, be accepted, be helpful, be the one who doesn't rock the boat… rather than, looking after our own needs?

It took me to the age of nearly forty to get completely conscious and realise how I completely drop my values and beliefs like a sack of potatoes to please people. I'd shove them aside to make sure others are emotionally okay and happy.

Unknowingly and unconsciously, being a people-pleaser was my top value and belief. It was my identity.

Looking back, there must have been a part of me who liked being a people-pleaser. Perhaps it made me feel validated, significant and special in some kind of way. I am going to admit something that sounds a bit wacky, but I think I was kind of holding out for a blue ribbon or high achievement award to frame on my wall. Something that says, 'For outstanding service, always thinking of others and people-pleasing to the max' signed, The Queen.

Yep told you it's a bit wacky… I wanted the Queen, her Royal Highness to recognise my worth. That I am a bloody hard worker and worked until my hands would bleed. My tired legs could hardly stand by the end of the week, bone ache was the norm by Friday, but I charged on. Not to mention, a yes lady, a devoted daughter, caring sister, loyal partner, loving mother, supportive friend, understanding boss, enthusiastic volunteer… I live to give!

This award never comes. Not even from my local Mayor. Nada. Nothing.

Through my study and wisdom as a Life Coach I now know that excessive people-pleasing can be a form of manipulation. It's manipulating people into liking us. Shessh, that's a worry.

What's even more of a worry is that so many people I know suffer with the same people-pleasing syndrome. We can get so caught up with the noises of the external world that we forget about our very own internal world - the one we get to live with until our last breath.

So it leaves me with these questions; Do we not love ourselves enough to just be… ourselves? Do we not love ourselves enough to speak up and look after our needs too? Do we not love ourselves enough to listen to our inner voice, our heart, telling us what we really want?

So, back to the moment my inner world was fighting. There I was, in the emergency department. I drove myself there which I shouldn't have really. I had extreme pain in my chest that felt like a strong hand was clutching my heart like one of those squeezy stress balls. Then my heart would kind of stop beating, only to start beating again and bounce around like a bouncy ball in my chest. My breathing was sharp and shallow, I felt shaky, faint and nauseous… something was not right.

When I arrived at the hospital, it was busy. We were still in the thick of the pandemic and I felt instantly extra worried that I am clogging up the medical system and I am overreacting. I like to downplay just in case I look like some hypochondriac fool. I mean, it was packed in the waiting area and there were people there with serious problems.

Nurses are such calm and wonderous people in my mind. The nurse asked me why I am here. 'Um I have heart pain, I feel really weird and unwell. I'm a little worried because my dad died of a sudden heart attack at a similar age…'

She nodded empathetically, took notes and then asked me if I had ever had any heart related symptoms before this event. 'No never, nothing like this before'. I could feel myself wanting to cry, the biggest lump was in my throat, because in that moment I realised the very reason I was in hospital, potentially with something quite serious, was because I silenced my values and beliefs. I didn't listen to myself. I didn't back myself. I put the louder voices first; Our society, the government, family and friends… their voices and their fears became so loud that I finally caved.

Just two days prior to this very moment, I got the jab. The one we all had to get to not be an outcast, to hold a job, to visit the doctor, to go to a concert. Every grain of me felt it wasn't for me (even though I totally respect what others decide to do). And so, there I was, as a result of that jab, laying there as the nurses and doctors got busy with all the big tests, toughing it out in extreme pain, questioning… is this the last day of my life?

I'm Still Standing

In the words of one of my favourite musical legends, Elton John, 'I'm still standing…yeah yeah yeah'.

I didn't die, thank goodness… but scared as hell and left wondering how to feel about all this.

I was released the next day with a host of issues, ongoing pain and suspected Myocarditis (inflammation of the heart muscle). That was later confirmed along with other inflammatory issues which I continue to navigate.

Golly gosh… once this lemon got squeezed, oh the juices that flowed. There were memories of so many situations where I recognised my commitment to pleasing others. Our society breeds us, especially women. We are indoctrinated into a system we didn't even know we signed up for. From this moment I had a sour (and sweet) taste in my mouth that I wanted to explore.

While I spent weeks recovering from the worst heart pain I've ever endured, I spent time thinking deeply about my situation. The fatigue and brain fog were really overwhelming at times, but when I turned inwards and listened, I gained more clarity and understanding of what I must do. Not should do, but must do.

I must listen to myself. Back myself. Love myself.

I must mention that I've had plenty of shit balls thrown my way over my lifetime (haven't we all) and the year I had in the lead up to this defining moment alone was surely enough to shake me by the shoulders and have me listen to the universe. I'd already experienced burnout a couple of months prior. I've had burnout many times in the past and 'soldiering on' is just what we do right? Let me rewind to the months leading up to the jab injury and paint the picture of my ignorance to self-love. I'll highlight how I didn't listen to myself and how now I do in the hope that this story shakes you (gently) by the shoulders.

My daughter was diagnosed with a nasty parasite that she'd been battling for years and after countless practitioners we decided to go with a gut specialist who recommended the ketogenic diet. In fact, after testing, it turned out my whole family had the parasite, so we all went onto a keto eating journey. 12 weeks of no sugar, no caffeine, no grains, no processed foods. We ate organic home-made everything – bone broth, meatballs, frittata, certain vegetables, cultured coconut yogurt, stews, soups, eggs any way you can imagine and fermented fruits. Getting yourself in ketosis is next level devotion of work in the kitchen (and sourcing the ingredients) but it worked for us after trying other conventional methods.

We starved off that pesky parasite but after 3 months of adding this extra 'master-chef' load and staying up late each night preparing food for the next day, it left me in a state of exhaustion. I could barely stand up some days. The kitchen, the place I loved to cook beautiful nourishing food for my family, became my least favourite place. I hated that kitchen, I hated cooking and I hated food shopping. Over a year has passed and me and the kitchen are only just starting to make friends again.

I run 2 businesses, I'm a wifey and I'm a mother of two beautiful young children. Up until recently, my main income is through my hairdressing studio where I have over one hundred regular loyal clients. This means, when the kids are at school, I'm working, constantly standing or walking. Then I do after school activities…

standing or walking. Then I'm in the kitchen… standing or walking. Then I'm doing the laundry, tidying or cleaning… standing or walking. You get the idea. I have an existing condition called Vascular Incompetence Disorder, in other words, sluggish blood flow to the veins in my legs. Excessive time on my feet creates huge problems… swelling, pain and throbbing. The warning signs were there, I kept pushing and pushing myself while I maintained the long days of running around. I couldn't possibly slow down, could I? My brain does not compute such thing.

Then, the day came, I could hardly walk. I could hardly do my job. I couldn't take great care of my family. My right leg was so painful, swollen and turning a bluish colour. I got in to see my vascular surgeon real fast and she said it's looking like a DVT (Deep Vein Thrombosis) which can be a serious blood clot that lodges in the vein. It needed to be operated on as soon as possible. She's a good lady, my Vascular surgeon, I know her well because she has lasered, stripped and injected my ongoing vein issues over numerous years. Off I went to hospital and Dr Anne did her magic. In recovery, she looked me square in the face and said 'You have got to give up hairdressing. You have got to give up standing so much. You must rest more often or you will end up with serious issues sooner than later.' I listened while almost choking up. I respect her so much, I knew she was right. I've been in a job constantly standing for the past 23 years… something had to change.

Knowing something had to change, yet there was that defiant voice… 'but, but what about your clients, you mustn't let them down, they need you!'

Part of me was so happy to take time off hairdressing, a job that I enjoy but the foundations of it are built on people-pleasing. It's a job of go, go, go, don't stop. I can link my yes-a-holic-ness back to my first boss, I call her 'dragon lady', for the fear of saying 'no' to people. She would sternly say 'you do not say no to me and you DO NOT EVER say no to a customer…got it?!' Gulp. Got it, Nicole can't say NO. Back then you didn't know your rights as an employee, that you could ring a fair work service to come investigate the total utter mistreatment. For example, lunch breaks were unheard of, finishing on time literally never happened, bonuses and fair pay was all over the shop, we'd never take a sickie day off, being told how to speak and how to dress was the norm. We had a system to follow; be nice as pie, bend over backwards, work your arse off, leave your troubles at the door and have a smile while you do it.

I worked there a long time with my fellow yes-a-holic colleagues. I became a yes lady without realising. Heck, I would even do people's hair at home on my only day off when all I really needed was rest. That way of being permeated into all parts of my life from the age of 17.

So while I rested my legs from the vein surgery in the tightest of tight support stockings, I poured my energy into my coaching business which was just taking off. It was so great to have time to sit at my computer and devote more time to life coaching, my dream job. As that month off ended I got a call from my mum to say my cousin had died. It was tragic. He took his own life. I went to his funeral the following week, and as his younger brother read his eulogy with so much heartfelt courage, I was only just keeping it together. My cousin was my age, he was far too young. It was heartbreaking to see he had wanted to end it all.

His one precious life, cut off too soon.

On the drive home from the funeral, I pulled up to some traffic lights that had just turned red. I took a quick glance in my rear-view mirror to discover a big 4WD vehicle was hurtling towards me at a decent speed. I braced myself and closed my eyes in anticipation for the impact… then, BOOM! My car was hit hard, rear-ended, and pushed into the car in front.

Reflection

In summary of these four months,

- Burnout - from staying up until 11 p.m. cooking each night (and hating my kitchen).
- Yes-a-holic syndrome – Constantly afraid to let others down, addicted to 'bending over backwards' and people pleasing.
- Painful vascular blockage in my leg – From overworking, standing and doing too much.
- Grief - Losing my cousin to suicide.
- Whiplash to my neck – Thanks to the guy driving his big car into mine.

And then…

To tie my story all together, a few weeks after all this was my jab injury. That's the moment I questioned everything.

I had a hard look at how I was doing life and who I was being. I had vivid memories flash before me like that 'This is Your Life' TV show.

Self-Love

I was reflecting on all the times I'd bypass my true thoughts and feelings for the comfort of others, or to do the 'right' thing.

I then reflected on the times I was brave. My heart started to feel lighter when I realised that I didn't always forget my values and beliefs. I value connection, fun, courage, creativity and adventure. I think I've been so busy that I hadn't stopped to reflect on the wonderful things I've achieved such as travelling the world, living in the UK, jumping out of planes, hiking 12 hours for charity, running successful businesses, regaining my health, making two little humans and maintaining beautiful bonds with loved ones. So if I've lived those values then why I add a new one to the top of my list? YES. A full body hell yes. Self-love has been added. To the top of my values list.

As the new, more conscious me emerges, I cherish what I have overcome… I feel a huge rush of self-love. Sure, I've been a people-pleaser most of my life. I'm proud of that journey… Now I'm ready to listen to myself daily.

Are you ready to listen to yourself too?

I declare: No more people pleasing (unless I want to) and way more self-love. No more exhausting myself and more balance. No more being influenced by the voices on the outside and way more trusting my voice within. No more saying yes when I really want to say no.

Furthermore, remembering that somewhere along the way I learned to become a yes-a-holic, and now it's time to unlearn. Nicole can say NO. And you can too.

Alicia Ann Wade

Boundaries

Boundaries are a necessary component of self-love. Without boundaries we can feel depleted, taken advantage of or feel intruded upon. Building healthy boundaries based on your own set of values and beliefs is essential for healthy relationships and ultimately a healthy life.

It's great to do thoughtful things, I love doing good and spreading kindness onto others. It's what everyone should be doing in my opinion. BUT it's when you are saying yes and people-pleasing at your own expense that is the problem.

If you keep doing the 'right thing', you would spend your life following someone else's directions instead of your own.

Remember how I said earlier that I started to become friends with the simple word 'no'? By giving myself permission to say no to things, not take everything on, draw a clear line for what is ok and not ok… It has been a total game-changer for my wellbeing.

You can be a good person with a kind heart and still say no to people. You cannot be everything to everyone.

When faced with a request or a situation, check in with yourself: Is your body feeling contractive or is it feeling expansive? If contractive, this is the time to listen to yourself.

Check in and ask 'what do I want?'. If expansive, and it feels good, go for it!

NO is a full sentence. When I started to say no to people, most of the time it went totally ok. In fact, they respected my honesty and wished me well. For those that showed disappointment or resistance to my 'no', it was uncomfortable, I nearly slipped back into old ways to make it all better. But I reminded myself of my boundaries and the greater good of my peace, my health, my energy, my precious family time… going back to that heart space won the mental battle.

One of the most important exercises you'll do as far as living a life full of self-love, and therefore generating better boundaries is getting rock solid on discovering your values and beliefs. Head on over to www.nicolepirrie.com under 'resources' and download the Self-Love workbooks – Mindfully go through the exercises, listen to what your heart says, and you will gain a blueprint of what you stand for. In this section you will also find a list of phrases to help you say no without sounding like a royal A-hole. Because after all, we want to strengthen relationships, not lose them!

Living with no regrets

Imagine you're having a cuppa with your eighty year old self. (If you're already eighty, I think you're amazing, please read on and imagine you're with your 100 year old self).

You and your wise old self have been chatting about life and she subtly suggests that staying true to you is the most important quest you can ever undertake. Self-love is living unapologetically you, so she shares the top 5 regrets of the dying*:

Alicia Ann Wade

1. I wish I'd had the courage to live a life true to myself, not the life others expected of me.

Does this one hit you right in the solar-plexus? I hope so.... Listen to yourself. Back yourself. Love yourself. Be the raw, honest and fullest expression of YOU.

2. I wish I hadn't worked so hard.

Yep, because as I mentioned, you end up exhausted and burnt-out. Balance is key.

3. I wish I'd had the courage to express my feelings.

Be brave to speak up, speak your truth. What's cool about this is it gives others permission to do so as well. With honesty, then comes vulnerability, then comes deeper connection, then comes love.

4. I wish I had stayed in touch with my friends.

True, real connection is what matters.

5. I wish that I had let myself be happier.

Just like happiness is a choice, so is feeling love for yourself. Let it in, feel it and soak in it. If not now, when?

Wisdom, a choccie biscuit and cup of tea go so well together don't you think? Take a moment to ponder the above, especially regret number one. It could change your life from this day forward.

What does self-love look like?

What does self-love look like for a recovering people-pleaser?

Well, from my experience it is quite liberating. It's dropping the guilt, it's letting go of the expectations you think people have of you, following your own path while spreading joy at the same time, loving yourself and loving others, it's knowing your values and beliefs… its living in alignment.

Most of all, when you learn that pleasing everyone is literally impossible… you become free.

If you need help with this, reach out for my one-on-one or group coaching program. I'll guide you through the inner work that dials up your self-love-o-metre so you can fast-track your way to your best damn life.

Here You Are

What if your heart was in charge? What does that voice inside truly want?

If we strip back the pleasing, the need to say yes, and the longing to be liked… What does your heart say? If we listen carefully, that voice inside is your compass, directing you to what you really want. Your heart knows the truth.

Sooner or later, you've got to bet on you. You've got to back yourself. You cheer for everyone else, you please everyone else, you support everyone else's endeavours, you work extra hours, you bake choc-chip cookies, you go to the 'save the tree's' rally…

It is time to please you. It is time to look in the mirror and love yourself. Here you are.

My mission and my deepest wish is for you to embody the following:

Self-love is stepping into your power whilst empowering others.

Self-love is shining your light and your love.

Self-love is trusting yourself and your needs.

Self-love is backing your thoughts and feelings.

Self-love is finding your voice and speaking your truth.

Self-love is listening to your heart.

Self-love is vulnerability, bravery and honesty.

Self-love is remembering how utterly incredible you are.

Self-love is going after what you really want.

Self-love is seeing yourself as whole and able.

Self-love is inspiring and shows others what's possible.

Self-love is the gift that keeps on giving.

Self-love is doing the things that bring you joy.

And finally,

Self-love is walking out the door with a twinkle in your eye, bringing ALL-OF-YOU-NESS, proclaiming 'I'm worth it, baby'....

Here YOU are.

Source:(List curated by palliative nurse and author Bonnie Ware – Titled: The Five Regrets Of the Dying, published 2011)

CHAPTER 8

Your Pathway to Self-Love

Kelly Kingston

"When we can have unconditional love for ourselves, we have unconditional love for everyone. My thoughts and healing love are with you!"

I see you
I hear you
I feel you
I acknowledge
I love you

When we can have unconditional love for ourselves we have unconditional love for everyone. My thoughts and healing love are with you!

THE FUTURE OF HEALING…
To be present in every moment.

Self-Love

What do we all want for our Lives? Most of us want to be happy and well, to live in "harmony and inner-peace"? Right….

When you are at peace within yourself, magic happen:

- You are more confident in your choices and spend less time seeking approval from others.
- You stop overeating, "binge-eating" or "emotional eating". You won't need these coping mechanisms.
- You will sleep better. Go to sleep easier and wake up feeling amazing.
- You think clearer and have more positive thoughts.
- Your body will not ache as much because you are holding emotions in your muscles and joints. Your body relaxes as it releases issues in your tissues.

In this crazy full life we lead, most of us have forgotten how to breathe, most people breathe in a very shallow breath that may cause tiredness, feeling inpatient and like you don't have much energy at all, and rightfully so. When I feel that I am out of sorts, I take on too much in my life with work, friends and family. The best thing that supports me is coming back to my breath…

Breathing

Our breath is our life force energy, it is the vital link between your physical body and your astral bodies.

Your breath is the key to increasing and mobilising this life energy. It will improve your vitality and concentration as well as supply the fuel that drives your healing powers.

It is important to avoid forcing results. This applies to all breathing techniques. If you feel discomfort or start to perspire you have missed the point of the exercise.

You are looking to achieve a restful and gentle space. So, if in doubt, please stop.

Let's do a process together of Breathing:

1. Find a quiet place to be alone, sitting in a comfortable posture, the spine straight. Or, lay down if you prefer.

2. Allow your eyes to close, if you like.

3. Become aware of your body and consciously allow every part of your body to relax.

    If you are struggling to relax your body, bring the awareness of your breath to your nostrils; feel your breath as it comes in and out of your nostrils. When you are fully aware of your breath, you have reached a relaxed space.

4. Take a deep breath in through your nose and think of your lungs as having 3 parts: a lower, a middle, and an upper space. Fill the bottom part of your lungs first, so that your stomach raises. Then, the middle… and finally, the top.

Now, release the air slowly and exhale a little bit more with a sigh, then start inhaling again and relax as you do this a few times.

5. Take a deep, unhurried breath and breathe to the following rhythm of 3:

   Inhale for 3, 1… and 2… and 3… now, hold for 3, 1… and 2… and 3…
   Now, exhale for 3, 1… and 2… and 3… Now hold for 3, 1… and 2… and 3…
   Repeat at least 3 times and then relax.

   If you are having trouble breathing this way, follow the rhythm as much as you can. Listen to your body and take a break when needed. Increase your breath when you feel you are ready.

   Do not cram the lungs with air to the point of discomfort; however, concentrate your full attention on what you are doing.

6. When you are ready, you can increase the count of each breath cycle:

   3 breaths → to 6 breaths → to 8 breaths… and beyond.

When you can master how to breathe again then you will release so much stress from your life with this one technique.

Alicia Ann Wade

Ok Story time;

When I was 32, I read my first book cover to cover, this was the first book I had read cover to cover in my life! I was told I was stupid because I couldn't read properly and every time I was asked to read out loud in class my heart would beat 10 times faster than it should. I would break out into a sweat and my voice became all shaky. This kept me in a limited belief system that I was not good enough to pick up my grades.

I really wanted to learn how to read properly but I was never given the opportunity to read what I wanted to read and to be totally honest I had no idea what I wanted to read which made it even harder for me.

In 2010 I started my first hobby business as a massage therapist and bio resonance specialist. I really loved what I did but I didn't understand business! This kept me in a limited belief system that I was not good enough to be a real business owner.

In 2012 I met my new business and life partner who happened to be an accountant. This amazing man taught me everything I needed to learn about business nationally and internationally. I became an international business strategist that supported small to medium businesses that wanted to grow their businesses internationally. Started my own charity organisation in 2015. I did this for just 5 years before my desire to step back into the healing and wellness space became so strong that if I continued to do what I did I would be so out of alignment with my true calling.

The next cycle of my professional business journey was to write my first book!!! OMGOSH I was going to be a book author. This excited me to no end. So I found a book coach and she worked alongside me for 12 months… I became #No 1 best-selling author in 2017 for my first book Your Ultimate Wellness Business Guide – What Frequency is Your Business Vibrating At?. This workbook is all about business planning for the heart for Wellness entrepreneurs who are stuck in their hobby business! I operated this business for 2 years and then found another gap that was missing in the wellness industry after immersing myself into health, healing and wellness expos. It soon became very obvious that a lot of wellness business owners were struggling to identify who they were in their life and business and who their target market was!! This stopped me in my tracks and left me gobsmacked that these gorgeous heart based business owners have massive personal trauma's and limiting beliefs to fully step into their business and have the confidence to speak their truth. They would speak about what they loved to do as a hobby business owner but they would not value their expertise for the information they were giving away for next to nothing at all.

So seeing this gap I couldn't turn and walk away, so I started to write my second book that ended up becoming a luxurious healing gift box called The **C**YCLE (**C**hange **Y**our **C**urrent **L**ife **E**xperience) aka A Retreat in a Box.

The retreat in a box is for women that are wanting to embrace changes in their life, but do not know how to sustain such changes. These women are going on retreats and are loving the experience of being on a retreat but they do not know how to sustain everything they learnt on the retreat and bring it into their day to day life…

This is where The CYCLE comes in. The CYCLE is your post retreat luxurious healing gift that supports and guides you into the world of change, and the best part is, it doesn't matter where you are in your life, or for what reason The CYCLE will support you every step of the way… Your next chosen cycle you choose for the direction of your future.

So it took me 3 years to bring my life's work to you!

So I hear you asking so how does it all work? Great Question. The Cycle will support you through a transitional healing journey, combining The 13 areas of Divine Interconnective, Colour Therapy, The Elementals, The 13 Chakra Systems, and 13 Crystals that have brought our WE THRIVE Jewellery Range alive.

Some areas are a visualisation concept to a physical and online process! The new business is called happy and well…

My main focus for happy and well is to create a true healing experience where you do not give your power and energy away, you claim it and women get to fully step into their self-healing journey to heal their traumas, triggers, ancestral patterns and limiting beliefs about who they think they are, so they can authentically step up and out into themselves to speak their truth and live their lives purpose with no speed bumps in the way!

This lifelong tool is for you to fully embrace life, embrace business (women sacred business) and embrace YOU! A true healing experience, self-assessing, self-led, with lots of self-care creating self-love which gets stronger each and every day.

Self-Love

What's in The Cycle I hear you asking me...

1. My Naked Skin Deep 180 pages Book - A Healing Guide that supports you to unleash your issues in your tissues to balance your feminine and masculine energies.
2. A Journal - To release what no-longer serves you.
3. 30 Day Vegetarian Meal Guide
4. 2 x Body Mantra posters
5. 42 Day Card Deck Pack - I See You Cards – Your Daily Guide for 42 Days
6. We Thrive Jewellery Range - 1 x Happy Crystal Mala Necklace 1 x Happy Crystal Bracelet - Hand crafted with no expense spared
7. An Honouring Self Agreement - To support speaking your truth and being authentic to self
8. Honouring Candle - To call in the light to start you on your healing journey.

As I have created The Cycle it has grown into a creation of its own, I can see so many other opportunities for this life changing sacred tool to support so many areas that would support making changes in your life that you are facing right now! You are guided by the I see you cards, a 42 card deck pack, every single day to support you releasing what no longer serves you! They say it takes 21 days to break a habit and 21 days to call in what you would like to receive, right now! So I created the 42 Day Change your Current Life Experience Challenge to allow this sacred new transformation to occur in your life when you choose to make changes in your life... There is no area of your life that The Cycle could not support you on your journey called life.

One of my favourite words is:

SELF – **S**oul **E**volving **L**ove **F**requency

The more you step into yourSELF the more clearer, confident and caring you become.

Did you know that there is an art to change? So many people attempt to make changes in their but do not know how to sustain these changes so here is a brief intro to The Art of Change. If you can remember these 4 words then you are halfway there. We combine these 4 words with colours.

The 4 words are Knowledge, Recognise, Realise and Potential here is a brief definition of each word for you.

1. **Knowledge**   *Unite with Self*
   a. You now knowledge and allow yourself to unite back with yourself.

Yellow: self-confidence, optimistic, happiness, mental energy, brightness.

Relates to the autonomic nervous system, also the pancreas and liver, clears toxins in the digestive system. It brings love and peace into your life; it is a purifying ray, very spiritual and the colour for meditation. The Chinese use it as the colour for mourning as they perceive yellow as a new dawn or rebirth, a new beginning.

2. **Recognise** *Give to Self*
   a. You now recognise and allow the process of giving back to yourself.

Purple: powerful, high ideals, inspiring, emotionally uplifting

Associated with the pituitary gland, governs hormones, assists the physical body as a whole, aids sleep, purifies the body and cleanses our deepest soul. Use with kidney problems, nervousness. It calms and soothes the mind, also the organs of sight, hearing, smelling, eyes, ears and nose.

3. **Realise** *Intention for Self*
   a. You now Realise with real-eyes that only you can set your own intention for yourself.

Green: balancing, harmonising, calming, soothing, comforting, relaxing

Links with the physical heart and blood circulation, seeks harmony and balance in life, is very refreshing to the body and spirit, and helps the emotional level. It is the colour for the nervous system, good for muscle spasms, a healing colour from the heart space, as it is after all nature's colour.

4. **Potential** *Detach from old Self*
   a. You now see your potential self and detach from your life what no longer serves you.

Blue: clarity, calming, soothing, protective, mental control, sedative

The healing ray calms both the positive and the negative electromagnetic links around the body. Excellent for epilepsy, fevers and inflammation, linked with the thyroid, vocal expression and verbal communication.

When you can master these 4 words and link them into change you will be able to make instant changes in your life without having to give this process to much thought at all.

Now, that you have the 4 secret words to The Art of Change we are then going to moving into the space of Your Voice Commands Your Mind, Body, and Spirit so now we have to bring attention and Awareness to what comes out of our mouth. The words we use are casting spells left, right, and centre and if you want to stay in the current life you have created for yourself then keep casting the same spells. If you want to make some serious changes in your life right now pay close attention to this area.

As you speak it, so it is.

Learn the true meaning of the words that you are commanding to you, around you and to the people you choose to be with every day... and how your words either empower you or take away your power.

Here is a powerful exercise for you.
Find the opposite word to each word, feel it, say it and do it, which one will move you forward and activate what you want more of in your life.

Help yourself by walking your truth for your own life and no-body else's. Keep thoughts, actions and words in alignment with your head held high facing your true north.

Be self-empowered!!
Be self - motivated!!
Be self-inspired!!
Be self-respectful!!

Phrases we choose Not To Use:

I can't = Cannot is a command to self
I won't = Will literally put a block in your way
It's hard = Will literally stop growth
I don't believe = Will literally stop you from achieving anything in your life
I'm a sceptic Is a taught behaviour that is a condition to hold a person back
I don't like it = Stops a person from learning, stops a person from gaining intellect

Try (Try and you will do it) Trying, I can try, I'm trying, I will try, I will attempt to try

Try is a command to Self = Try and Trying is a taught behaviour that is a condition to hold a person back, it has very very little result, it's like running a race with no end, never ending, it is repetitious.

Help yourself by walking your absolute truth of your life. Keep thoughts, actions and words positive.

Be self-empowered.

Phrases To Use

I can = Literally promotes growth, can is a command to self.
I am = Believing in your full ability.
I believe = Allows your wants, needs and desires to come true.
It is done = Is a behaviour of stamping in what you have asked for.
I can do it = Is unconditional and can move a person forward in life.
I can do anything = When you know you can do it and your body needs to hear it. Your body reacts to key words.

Un-happy Inner Child

- Plays the Victim role
- Insecure with Self
- Needs external validation
- Afraid to be alone
- Easily Triggered
- Always very serious
- Looks for the negative in everything
- Filled with stress and worry

Happy Inner Child

- Takes ownership
- Feels confident and secure
- Enjoys being alone
- Calm and understanding
- Creates joy and happiness
- Finds the positivity in everything
- Filled with light and love
- What other people think about you is none of your business. Your business is to focus on your own growth and healing. It's all about minding your own business.

And last but not lest as you grow stronger in all areas of your life emotionally, mentally, spiritually and environmentally we need to put equal focus on the physical, feeding your body temple with a balanced meal planner that supports you not having to think about what you need to plan for your week or month ahead, we have your back and this is all sorted for you…

A vegetarian meal guide that supports how you want to feel everyday of your life. If you feel you cannot give up meat you can cook the meat of your choice into the meal you are preparing and slowly remove meat altogether, or not. The beautiful thing about this whole process you have the final say!

If anyone would like a copy of my 7 day meal guide please go to my website and subscribe and it will be emailed to you within minutes.

When we are more aware of what we put into our bodies we are more aware of our bodies….

And this to me all your beautiful souls is how I see The Future of Healing taking full responsibility for our life… ♡

CHAPTER 9

Titin I Forgot

Titin Mubarokah

"True self-care is not bath salts and chocolate cake; it's making the choice to build a life you don't need to escape from." – Brianna Wiest

"Titin, can you hear me? Titin, can you hear me?"

"She is not responding"

"Hello Titin, can you hear me?" No, she can't hear us."

"She still not responding, call an ambulance quickly"

"Check her breathing, can you feel her breath?"

"She is not breathing; she is not breathing"

"Get someone to do the CPR on her and get the defibrillator"

"Keep checking on her breath"

"Is she breathing now?"

"Check her blood level"

"Check her heart rate"

"We need to bring her to the hospital"

It was a chaotic scene, they said.

Something that people weren't expecting for Friday morning at the office lobby.

Paramedics and a few people from work surrounded me and tried to help me so I could breathe normally and gain consciousness.

Meanwhile, I could almost hear everything yet my whole body was paralyzed, I could not even open my eyes or respond.

My whole body and muscles felt so weak.

I could not talk, I'm speechless. I can barely move my body anymore.

I was unconscious for about a minute and had no idea what was going on.

That morning, I woke up feeling a bit tired and weak.

I told myself, "I'm fine, I should get up and take a shower."

"Perhaps because I didn't get much sleep last night," "I can't take a day off"

Despite usually taking the tram, I was able to drive to work.

I made a concerted effort to focus on my work as soon as I arrived at the office. From there, everything deteriorated rapidly. I'm almost shivering from exhaustion, and I'm feeling so cold that my vision is also starting to fade.

"I need something to boost my energy, I will buy myself some effervescent vitamins and let myself have some ice cream too"

I went downstairs and walked to the nearby convenience shop to get the ice cream and look for a pharmacy to get the vitamins. You can bet that craving was out of the ordinary and uncharacteristic of me because I never ate ice cream in the morning.

As I walked onto the street, I was quite scared of how my body felt at that time, it was weird, kind of like floating. Then, I'm walking to the place inside one of the buildings that I thought was the pharmacy. When I realised I had gone to the wrong location because there are no shops there, I became perplexed. Instead, I ended up in childcare! It appears that the pharmacy business and childcare have the same name. Because I didn't read the entire signage in the front building, I had assumed it must be a pharmacy when I entered the daycare. When I came out of the building, I tried to read the signage again, and of course, it said childcare under the shop name. I was as bad as that. I made a lot of effort to focus while reassuring myself that everything would be fine. Instead, I continued to walk to the other store to purchase the ice cream in the hopes that it would at least give me a sugar rush.

I was even more worn out, baffled, blank, and getting weaker by the minute when I returned to the office. The ice cream didn't even help my energy level as it normally would.

At this point, I was aware that something was wrong with my body and that I needed to take action.

I was mistaken, though, because I kept telling myself, "I'll be fine later; all I need to do is have a little lie down in the car and I'll be fine again, then I can come back to the office."

I made a feeble attempt to call my friend, asking her to meet me at the lobby office and drive me to my car in case I was unable to do so on my own.

I started to feel weaker and eventually passed out while waiting for her, but little did I know that things would only get worse from there.

I was lying in a hospital bed the next thing I realised. I had an IV, a blood oxygen monitor in one arm, a blood pressure cuff on the other, and cables dangling from my body to monitor my heart rate.

That was a terrifying wake-up call for me, but it wasn't the first time it had happened. A similar occurrence happened to me about five years ago...

This one is unquestionably the worst because, according to them, I wasn't breathing.

My body was very depleted because I had hypoglycemia, also known as "hypo" and low iron levels.

Hypoglycemia is a condition where your blood sugar (glucose) level drops too low. There are two main categories, according to Wikipedia.

The first group of symptoms is known as neuroglycopenic symptoms and results from low brain glucose.

Adrenergic symptoms, which are the body's response to low blood sugar in the brain, make up the second category of symptoms.

In my case, the symptom I experienced falls into the first category, which is neuroglycopenic symptoms. These include headaches, blurred vision, tiredness, confusion, lightheadedness, difficulty speaking, and passing out.

I am incredibly grateful to be alive today because severe hypoglycemia can be fatal. By quickly pumping glucose into my blood through the IV, the paramedics were able to raise my blood sugar levels. The fact that I don't have diabetes or an eating disorder made it impossible for me to believe when I read about the low blood sugar levels.

I came to the conclusion that my diet wasn't balanced. I've been too preoccupied to think about anything else besides how much fruit and vegetables I consume. Being Asian, I used to consume a lot of rice during the day, but over the past few years, I have changed this.

Self-Love

I was consuming progressively less rice and other carbs. I also came to the realisation that I had been exercising more recently than usual, assuming that the more exercise I get, the more energy I have, while oblivious to the need to balance my dietary intake. My body uses glucose more now that I'm exercising more, especially my muscles. I only weigh 52 kg and am a vegetarian, so I don't accumulate a lot of body fat or muscle.

Once more, I have neglected to take care of and love myself.

I had never worked in sales before, but six months ago I accepted a full-time position as a home loan consultant. Being a single mother at the time, I had to do this to support both my daughter and myself. Even though I work as an empowerment and well-being coach part-time, I still need a steady main income to support my family.

I wanted a better life for myself and my daughter without relying on anyone else. I wanted to buy our dream house and live comfortably. I wanted to build a yoga retreat in Bali and have my own business without worrying about money.

I was the only woman consultant in my department at work. Being the only female and one of the older individuals there gave me another incentive to excel and to demonstrate to myself that I can compete with them.

"I have to be one of the best performers at work amongst these young men," I said to myself.

I was being overpowered by masculine energy and assimilating it into myself.

I had a 5.30 a.m. wake-up time every day. I would do yoga, have quick breakfast, and study before going to work. On most days, I skip breaks and eat a late lunch. I would prepare dinner for my daughter and me, coach my client, or participate in webinars if any are offered, stay up late sleeping, and repeat the process the following day.

I was in a rush every single day. I was too obsessed with making money and having a good reputation at work.

I forgot to look after my mind and my body.

I forgot to have regular rest and take deep breaths when I could.

I forgot to nourish myself with good food.

I forgot to acknowledge and celebrate myself for my achievements.

I forgot to remind myself that I have everything I need right now.

I forgot to remind myself that I am where I am supposed to be.

I forgot to remind myself that I don't have to be scared of life.

Yes, I love my job.

Yes, I did very well at work.

Yes, I consistently demonstrated that I was capable of being one of the team's best players.

I have therefore neglected to consider my well-being.

I was once more paying a lot of attention to my surroundings.

In addition to being a mother and running my coaching business, I was exhausting myself at work.

This incident served as a further prompt for me to pause, evaluate my situation, and alter how I was approaching how I wanted my life to be. Once more, I've grown from my mistakes.

Instead of prioritising busyness, I need to prioritise self-care, self-love, and enjoying the "NOW."

My coaching clients learn these things from me.

I must, however, once more walk the talk.

But I've neglected to apply them to myself. And that's okay. Nobody is perfect; all I need is a reminder to start over.

Self-care and self-love are all I need. It doesn't mean I have to take a bath or treat myself to my favourite dessert every day. Or buying myself expensive clothing and handbags to make me feel good. There is internal care involved in addition to external care.

The day after the event, I was forced to take some days off, and I used that to do some reflection and planning to align my mind, my body, and my spirit.

I started by analysing the situation I was in and writing down a few ideas for how I would prefer it to be and why that was important to me. These include the list of daily self-love and self-care activities, as well as the list for the weekend. I emphasise putting my needs first.

I wrote about my updated objectives, the specific results I desire, and my perspectives on achieving them. I discussed potential challenges to achieving my objectives in my writing. For accountability, I talked about my new objectives with my coach and a select group of my close friends. They would check on me occasionally to see my progress.

I had a couple of sessions with my coach to discuss my old traumas and emotional wounds and work towards healing them. Since I haven't fully recovered from these wounds, I realised they were still having an impact on my life (or at least some aspect of it). Although this occurred when I was very young, I was unconsciously living in that period. I scheduled a visit with my doctor, had my blood tested, and talked about my health.

I started doing meditation right before bedtime every night. My mental clarity and sleep schedule are both improved by this step. I've added journaling to my morning routine because it has previously assisted me in getting rid of pointless thoughts and ideas rather than letting them stew in my head all day.

During the day, I would be checking my feelings and emotions so I could fully express them and regulate them if needed. I would practise my deep breathing, positive affirmation, and positive self-talk and watch my thoughts as many times as I could. ensuring that I would recognise my negative thought and replace it with gratitude.

I started eating more mindfully, maintaining a more balanced diet that included foods high in iron and protein, nourishing myself with good-quality, organic produce, keeping myself hydrated with water throughout the day, and most importantly, taking periodic breaks during the day.

My body and mind have been reset by following these steps. I feel more aligned and feel the love I am giving to myself.

I know I have one body and one life. I am so grateful, and I would not waste that. I would not take my life for granted again and create unnecessary suffering. It would be silly to lose my life because I was overworked and did not look after myself for the sake of money and security.

I realised that putting myself first is not selfish; after taking care of myself, I can take care of others. I wouldn't want to feel the consequences if I neglected and forgot to take care of myself again.

My emotional health and well-being are as important as my physical health, as this affects my relationships with others.

I promise myself for the second time to practice self-love, to be kind to myself, make priorities, identify my needs, and make sure they are met so that I don't burn myself out again.

Yes, life is unpredictable sometimes, and it can be scary. Especially if you have been through a lot in life.

How I see life is like a Ferris wheel, always turning; it will never stop revolving. Sometimes the wheel is on top, and sometimes it is on the bottom. We might as well enjoy the ride instead of overthinking and fearing what will happen next.

The question is: if you know that they are always turning, how do you ride the Ferris wheel? Do you ride with enjoyment and fun? Or fear of falling?

In my view, if I ride my Ferris wheel in fear, I will miss the fun life and regret it later. This is the same as wishing for the perfect time to be happy and enjoy life when I reach a certain amount of money. I realised that there is no perfect time, the time is now, not in the future, not in the past, but now

Echart Tolle says: "As soon as you honour the present moment, all unhappiness and struggle dissolve, and life begins to flow with joy and ease. When you act out of moment-to-moment awareness, whatever you do becomes imbued with a sense of quality, care, and love—even the simplest action."

This is a fundamental component of my self-love routine. Focusing on the here and now and taking in everything and all the beauty around me. One of the remarkable things for me is that each time I'm in the present moment and enjoying my own time, I always see the heart shape in any form, it could be in a form of a rock, leaf, flower, or even a drop of water!

Each time I saw those heart shapes, I felt a sense of joy sweep over me. I know that I'm okay and that I'm on the right path. At that moment, I would put my hand on my heart and give thanks and

Self-Love

gratitude for the fact that I am healthy, I am happy, and I have everything in life.

Life is a journey, not a destination. As human beings, of course, we forget sometimes, and that's okay too. We just need a reminder.

Here is the list of the self-love routines I used:

Have a regular short break and add in 10 minutes of body scan meditation at least once a day.

Balance my diet by adding carbohydrates, fibre, proteins, and iron-rich food.

Drink plenty of water during the day.

Listening to my favourite music, dancing, and having fun as much as I can.

Adding meditation as part of my daily routine.

Journalling.

Checking in with my coach every week.

Acknowledge and celebrate myself whenever I achieve something.

Positive self-talk and affirmation every day.

Planning my week every Sunday, including the meal plan.

Expressing myself and my emotions, letting emotions out, cry when needed.

Knowing my self-worth and respecting myself.

Respect my boundaries, know my needs and. know when to say no.

Knowing that putting myself first is not selfish.

Take a little nap on the weekend when needed.

Schedule to visit nature at least once a month.

A barefoot walk on the grass whenever I can.

Bathe every Sunday night before bed or when I'm tired or overworked.

Exercise every day for a minimum of 30 minutes, this can be as simple as walking, running, yoga, dancing, etc.

Doing the things I love on the weekend (including bouldering!)

Schedule a massage every 3 weeks or so.

Now, I have recovered completely from my low blood sugar and low iron level by having an iron infusion, aside from monitoring and managing my blood sugar with a properly balanced diet.

My body is my temple, and I have one responsibility to give it as much love and care as anyone else will.

"Healthy self-love means being gentle with the soul within you. To love oneself is the purest, bravest thing. Anyone in the entire world can experience self-love. Just do the simple acts of love for yourself, and then your authentic self begins." – Anonymous

These are the affirmations I read when I wake up in the morning:

I wake up with a peaceful mind and a grateful heart

I open my eyes to the wonder of nature

I greet the day with ease

I will not worry about things I cannot control

I am in charge of my thoughts

I am worthy of love

I am grateful for who I am and who I can be

I am enough

I accept myself

I am a magnet for the experiences I most desire

All I need comes to me at the right time

I give and receive love, joy, and kindness

I welcome chances to help those in need

Alicia Ann Wade

I acknowledge help and guidance when given

I am thankful for this life and its opportunity

I am humble in my success and praise others

I am grateful for all that I have

I am enough, I am loved, and I am where I am supposed to be.

Much Love and gratitude,
Titin
Head over to my website for some free resources
titincoachingandwellness.com
Titin Mubarokah | Holistic Counsellor & Empowerment Coach
W: titincoachingandwellness.com
E: contact@titincoachingandwellness.com

CHAPTER 10

The Tree That Learned To Blossom

Alpa Sancheti

"The path to self-acceptance and love is not a simple one, I am aware of that. It requires effort, commitment, and the courage to face our fears and apprehensions."

How did I end up in this situation?

I stood frozen in front of the door with my hand tethered to the doorknob, desperately trying to think of the answer. And at that precise moment, I judged myself a loser and a failure. I had lost my dreams along with my identity, voice, and sense of worth. I resembled a tree that had lost all of its leaves and was now exposed to the elements of the outside world. It was agonising to realise that the life I had worked so hard to create had been shattered into a million pieces. On the one hand, I was sinking into a sea of self-doubt, self-blame, and resentment; on the other, a part of me was racked with pain and anger. I was suffocating under the weight of the emotions

I was carrying. Despite my efforts to make sense of it all, the pain was too great to bear.

Even now, I can still remember the heaviness in my chest, the tears streaming down my terrified face, and the sound of my trembling voice trying to dissuade me from what I was about to do. I was aware that the moment I exited that door, I would be on my own and unable to access the doors of what society would consider to be safe. However, I knew deep down that I had to leave, that I could no longer pretend to be alive or put up with anyone treating me disrespectfully.

I was at a fork in the road where one path led back to the security of familiarity and the other led into the unknown, the latter of which might bring about the fulfilment of my worst fear. How could I decide between the security of the known and what lay ahead? Was I prepared to confront my worst anxieties and find the hidden truths inside of me? Was I willing to explore uncharted territory?

Have you ever encountered a crossroads in your life? How did you decide which course to follow?

Better the devil you know than the angel you don't know?

Sometimes in life, things happen that make us doubt our existence, challenge our beliefs, and put strengths we didn't know we had to the test.

And for me, it was the day I made the decision to leave my marriage and my ex-partner's home with nothing more than a bag of clothes, all alone in a foreign country without any family. Even if they had wanted to, my family and close friends who were my rock could not have travelled to be with me as I broke because they lived so far away. However, I was no longer willing to put up with any more humiliation, disrespect, or control. His deception served as a final blow to me.

I was extremely hurt, perplexed, and wondering what I did wrong. For a very long time, I simply kept making sacrifices, putting others before myself, striving for perfection, keeping quiet to avoid arguments, projecting the image of a happily married wife in public, and compromising my morals in order to win others' love, acceptance, and respect. But as I stood there, hurt and alone, I understood that my entire life had been a lie. Years of searching for acceptance and love had only brought me to this point of hopelessness. It was like I had been walking down a road that I thought was leading me to my dreams, only to realise too late that it was a dead end. The worst part was that I had no idea why.

In my quest for love, I transformed into a shell of the person I once was, lacking confidence and feeling completely powerless. I hardly recognised this new version of myself. I was just going through the motions of each day without any real purpose or direction because I had lost sight of what I wanted out of life. I experienced a crushing sense of defeat as a result of it. The pain of staying was too great to bear, even though I had no idea where I was going or what would happen next. The road ahead was cloudy and uncertain. I was aware that I had to decide between being the person I was and the person I could be. I could feel the weight of my choice pressing in on me, threatening to extinguish the meagre glimmer of hope to which I was clinging. I yearned to connect with that spark, to allow it to ignite and lead me to a more promising future. However, in order to do that I had to let go of the safety net that had kept me imprisoned for so long.

My hand trembled with fear as I reached for the doorknob. The familiar voice in my head begged me once more to remain put to preserve the delusion of safety and normality that I had clung to for such a long time. And amongst that chaos of emotions and fear, I could also hear a separate, tiny voice of my sister, reiterating to me the words of Elizabeth Gilbert from her book Eat, Pray, Love, "You've gotta stop wearing your wishbone where your backbone ought to be." It was time for me to develop a strong backbone, stand up for myself, and lead the life I deserved. With a deep breath and a final look around the room, I opened the door and stepped out of that door, out of that relationship and out of that life. And as I ventured into the unknown, I concluded that the only thing more terrifying than the outside world was the idea of leading a life devoid of who I truly am.

The days that followed weren't exactly simple. Even after I left, there was still internal unrest, and I was intimidated by my demons. The hardest part was learning to forgive myself and overcoming my pain, fear, confusion, and inner critic. They had evolved into a kind of constant companion who would never abandon me, in particular, my inner critic. I agree that we all have an inner voice that just won't stop talking, offering unsolicited opinions, suggestions, and remarks while occasionally muttering, "Not good enough." But for me, that voice was more akin to a Dementor from the Harry Potter series; it affected both my personal and professional lives, draining my soul and leaving me feeling like a hollow shell. Everything about me became tainted by it, including my thoughts and deeds. I consequently made decisions that I wasn't always happy with or that were in my best interests.

I could still hear this voice saying things like, "You're not smart enough, pretty enough, talented enough, or worthy enough." The list is endless. Every time I tried to decide for myself, the voice buzzed even louder in my ear, making me doubt my judgement and second-guess my choices. Taunting me by constantly bringing up the mistakes I've made in the past and the suffering I've caused my mother, my family, and myself.

Has your inner critic ever haunted you, leaving you with self-doubt and uncertainty about your abilities and choices? If so, what effect has it had on your life?

Did you go down in a spiral of shame and self-doubt like I did?

I was never able to pinpoint how I changed into someone who put up with so much abuse. It was as if I were travelling through a thick fog, as I was unable to see the path I was taking or the location I was going. I had strong opinions about how women should be respected, and was generally self-assured, but here I was: a victim of emotional abuse. I realised that, like a carton of milk left unopened in the refrigerator, our relationship had long since expired. It had spoiled, turned sour, and was now wholly poisonous. But even though it had passed its expiration date and I knew in my heart that it was harming me, humiliating me, and eroding my self-respect, I clung to it tightly and couldn't bring myself to let go. Why did I allow it to happen? How could I accept something harmful to me?

Alicia Ann Wade

Have you ever found yourself settling for less, staying put in a relationship, or holding yourself back from pursuing what you truly deserve in your professional or personal life?

Is it because you feel deserving of it, or because you fear being alone, failing, being rejected, being judged, not being loved, not being good enough, or just the unknown?

I pondered what caused me to feel so inadequate. Was it the guilt I felt for betraying my mother by choosing to live my life with my ex-partner despite her warning me about all the red flags in our relationship, which I was blind to; or was it the rose-coloured glasses I wore, which distorted everything through optimism rather than the reality of what it is; or was it some other factor? At the time, I was at a loss for words. However, I stayed up for many nights worrying about these questions. While trying to make sense of it all, I stumbled upon a study. The research discussed how co-dependent behavior, often characterized by maintaining unhealthy relationships out of loneliness or fear of abandonment, can lead to low self-worth and feelings of shame. My feelings of shame and unworthiness were made more understandable in some ways, but there were still so many unanswered questions. I started my journey of self-discovery and self-healing out of a desire to learn more about who I truly am and to rid myself of the pain.

I once read that a thousand-mile journey starts with a single step. But let me tell you, my journey to self-discovery felt more like a journey of a million steps, with plenty of wrong turns and stubbed toes along the way.

It wasn't simple, and there were many obstacles to overcome. It would be an understatement to say that accepting every aspect of who I am—the good, the bad, the ugly, and every shade in between—was the hardest part. The most terrifying thing, in the words of renowned psychoanalyst Carl Jung, is to accept oneself completely. If I were to map my progress it would appear more like a heartbeat graph than a straight line. Fortunately, I had the backing of friends, family, and a coach who had faith in me and recognised my authentic self when I struggled to do so.

Though the burden of my past mistakes weighed heavily upon my shoulders, threatening to crush me under its weight. But this time I was not ready to let my inner demons suck the life out of me. This time, I refused to be defeated. With each passing day, I grew stronger, more resilient, and more determined to break free from the chains that bound me to my insecurities.

When I look back, I see that I thought I had it all figured out: be the good girl, make everyone happy, don't mess up, obey, only see the best in people, and stay out of trouble. And by doing these things I will always be accepted and loved. Like I was when I was a kid and a girl. My younger self had a reputation for being obedient, performing well in school, and staying out of trouble. My parents beamed with pride, my teachers held me in high esteem, and I firmly believed I had cracked the code of life and was doing everything just right, as I was the star in their eyes. And to tell you the truth, I loved the praise and validation that came with being a "good girl," and I started to believe that was what I was supposed to be. Before I knew it, I had a burning desire to be the ideal friend, partner, daughter, sister, student, and, eventually, a person that everyone would accept and love.

Have you ever fallen into the trap of trying to be perfect or the one who never makes mistakes and is loved and accepted by all?

I was unaware that maintaining the "good girl" persona and the associated beliefs simply caused me to disconnect with my inner self and repress my own needs, wants, and emotions. I had no idea that this behaviour was feeding a snake of inner emptiness and unhappiness that would only serve to exacerbate my life's experiences of low self-worth and shame. It took me years and hitting rock bottom for me to understand that this "good girl" mindset could not last and was doing more harm than good. I gradually unpacked and altered these ingrained patterns and beliefs that had been preventing me from moving forwards for so long with the assistance of my coach.

As I delved deeper into this new chapter of my life, I realised that cultivating a positive relationship with oneself, which is nothing other than self-love, is the secret to healing and personal growth. When I first learned about the concept of self-love, this was completely at odds with what I thought it meant. I had this false notion that self-love equated to selfishness and self-centeredness. I was so mistaken, though.

As I started diving deeper into understanding self- love, I realized self-compassion is the first step in developing self-love. The concept of self compassion given by psychologist and author Dr Kristin Neff resonated with me. Giving ourselves the same kindness that we would extend to others is what self-compassion is all about. Yet, it is funny and tragic both that we feel okay putting conditions on loving ourselves. It is so simple for us to love and accept others while ignoring their flaws, errors, failures, and other issues. And when it comes to us, we look at ourselves through a magnifying glass that accentuates all our flaws, errors, and failures. Simply put, we are unable to accept and love ourselves completely for who we are and what we contribute to the world.

Being compassionate with myself and accepting that I'm not perfect, that I make mistakes, and that those mistakes don't define who I am was one of the hardest lessons I had to learn. I had already forgiven him when I left my ex-partner's home. However, it took me a long time to forgive myself and realise that making a mistake does not automatically make me a failure or a bad person. It does not imply that I am unworthy of love and support or that I cannot ask for assistance. To avoid mistakes, I do not need to strive for perfection and, in the process, lose myself or equate being vulnerable with being imperfect and weak. I made a deliberate effort to practise self-compassion, treating myself with the same benevolence and compassion that I would extend to a close friend, and to keep going.

By practising self compassion and self love I was able to accept and appreciate myself for who I am, including my past mistakes and imperfections. It also empowered me to make better choices for myself, prioritizing my well-being and happiness.

To nurture self-love, I also focused on self-care, dedicating time and energy to activities that nourished my mind, body, and soul. By honouring my needs and desires without condemnation or guilt, I was able to connect with myself on a deeper level. This connection made it possible for me to explore inner child work, a therapeutic strategy developed by psychologist John Bradshaw that focuses on mending the emotional scars from our past and tending to the needs of our inner child.

As my self-love and inner child work grew, I found it simpler to forgive myself for the hurt I had caused my family and for betraying my own needs by remaining in a toxic situation for so long. With a newfound sense of self-acceptance and self-worth, I could finally let go of my guilt and embrace the opportunities that awaited me in this new phase of my life.

Little did I realize that one day, this personal journey would grant me a renewed sense of empowerment, igniting my curiosity to delve deeper into the study of human relationships and behaviors. Not only did it lead to the incredible results I achieved, but it also became an indispensable part of the work I now do in supporting and assisting others.

I consistently attended my coaching sessions, put in the necessary effort, read books, and worked on myself, which allowed me to gradually peel back layers of shame, low self-worth, and self-doubt. I discovered how to be kind to myself, stand up for myself, create a loving relationship with myself, and ask for assistance when I needed it.

The road to self-love was winding and long, but in the end, it was worth every twist and turn. For now, I stand tall, unafraid to face the world, secure in the knowledge that I am enough, just as I am. My story is not about a superhero who was born to do something great or was always right, but about a normal girl who made mistakes, repeated them, failed, got hurt, and hurt those she loved. However, she eventually learned to blossom like a tree into the person she was always meant to be. As I opened up about my experiences, I discovered that many of them resonated with those who had faced similar challenges. Owning our story can be challenging, but it's not nearly as challenging as living our lives in denial about it, such an eloquent reminder by Brené Brown. By embracing vulnerability and owning my story, I hope to encourage others on their path to healing, self-love, and ultimately the freedom to live authentically and fully.

The path to self-acceptance and love is not a simple one, I am aware of that. It requires effort, commitment, and the courage to face our fears and apprehensions. And I can vouch that with the right support and mindset, we can overcome even the toughest challenges and emerge stronger than ever before. I am living proof of that, and I know that I will continue to grow and thrive in the years to come. I wholeheartedly desire the same for others too.

And for those individuals who are ready to embark on the beautiful journey of self-love, I extend my guidance and support. My goal is to assist them in exploring the depths of their inner world and unleashing their boundless potential, allowing them to create a more fulfilling, authentic, and meaningful life.

So today, let's take the first step towards cultivating a deeper sense of self-love by incorporating these three transformative actions into our daily routines. Each step is designed to empower us to embrace our worthiness and prioritize our well-being.

1. Break free : Get clear on what you are no longer willing to accept. Take a moment to reflect on the aspects of your life that no longer serve you or align with your values. Identify any patterns, behaviors, or relationships that no longer serve you. By recognizing and acknowledging what you are no longer willing to accept, you take the first step towards setting boundaries and honoring your self-worth.

2. Nurture : Prioritize self-care and self-nurturing. Make a conscious effort to dedicate time each day to activities that bring you joy, peace, and rejuvenation. Whether it's practicing mindfulness, indulging in a hobby, or simply taking a relaxing bath. Prioritizing self-care sends a powerful message that you value yourself and deserve to be nurtured.

3. Cultivate: Practice self-compassion and positive self-talk. Be kind and gentle with yourself, especially in moments of self-doubt or setbacks. Cultivate a loving inner dialogue, replacing self-criticism with self-compassion. Celebrate your accomplishments, acknowledge your strengths, and embrace your uniqueness. This shift in mindset help reshape your self-image and cultivate a deeper sense of love and acceptance for yourself.

These steps have been instrumental in my personal transformation and continue to be a vital part of my daily routine. Feel free to adapt them to suit your unique needs and preferences, and be compassionate with yourself if you're unable to check off every item every day. The ultimate goal is to consistently practice self-love and integrate it into your daily routine. Self-love is not a one-time or temporary act, but rather a daily practice that extends throughout the entirety of our lives.

I'd like to leave you with one of my favourite lines from writer and artist Topher Kearby. "You became who you needed to be in order to survive. But now it's time to become who you need to be so you can thrive in life. Change is coming. It's time to embrace it"

P.S.
If you're ready to transform your relationship with yourself and step into your power, or if you'd like to share your story or thoughts on what resonated with you from my journey, I would be thrilled to hear from you. Let's connect on
Instagram - www.instagram.com/transcendingyou
Facebook - https://www.facebook.com/Transcendingbeyond.with.alpa
Website - www.transcendingyou.com.au

I'd also like to give you free access to my self-love meditation as a way of showing my gratitude. You can start developing a stronger sense of self-acceptance and self-compassion by using this effective tool. Visit my website to get access to this freebie and additional resources.

I'm excited to get to know you and be there for you as you travel down your own path to healing, growth, and self-awareness.

CHAPTER 11

Grief, the highest form of Self-Love

Tasha Dziesinski

"After hitting rock bottom, I grew to love myself despite the suffering. It was empowering to learn that all this time, I was my own hero."

What do you mean by "grief is the highest form of self-love?" I can already hear you asking. Isn't grief very painful, demanding that we let go of someone or something we care about? Yes, that's true, but it also gives us the chance to discover how to love ourselves even during the most trying times.

I was recently asked what self-love meant to me. I replied, "It's a journey," in response. We never reach a finish line and declare, "Okay, I'm here!" It's a continuous, intentional journey. I, myself, seemed to have found self-love during a very tough time.

I'm going to go on a journey with you today. Imagine having everything you knew placed in a paper bag, shaken up quickly, and then dumped out on the floor. I felt as though this had occurred to me. My heart was broken to pieces, and I was left trying to put all the pieces back together. This is my story.

Early in 2019, I reached a turning point where the hurt and pain from my past finally emerged from the numbness. I suddenly started feeling again. I started experiencing panic attacks and flashbacks because it was so overwhelming. At first, I had no clue where this was all coming from or why it was happening. I would eventually come to understand that it resulted from repressed and suppressed emotions as well as living automatically. After years of entanglement and self-ignorance, I finally felt the effects of my actions. I had no clue who I was.

I experienced severe depression in early 2020, during a global pandemic. I locked myself in my room and wouldn't leave when I wasn't working. Sometimes, I didn't even come out to eat. I felt as though I was just existing. I was imprisoned in this anxiety-filled, self-deprecating, and self-critical pit of darkness. I had always allowed it to define me. I mistakenly believed that was just the way I was and the way things were. Although I was aware of what I was thinking and feeling, I was unsure of how to escape.

I became a member of an online membership community in June 2020. I had, at last, realised that I needed assistance. I decided to give myself a membership as a birthday present. I've made friends with people from all over the world thanks to this community.

As I began my work in this community, I started to learn how to catch unhelpful thoughts and about self-compassion and self-care. I started educating myself on how to improve my relationship with myself. I initially found a lot of this to be very difficult. Being kind to myself was something that I found incredibly difficult to accept. It didn't seem to make sense to me. I thought it would only make me soft and cause me to fail. I now understand that failure is unavoidable. We all fail from time to time. When I experienced a setback, I was treating myself in a way that required improvement.

I did start moving slowly forward with the work, but I was still having a lot of trouble regulating my emotions when I was triggered. Additionally, I was still having a lot of trouble with negative self-talk and criticism. Every time I was triggered or faced a challenge, I felt ashamed of myself. But I continued to post in the group and ask for help when I needed it. I kept showing up for the classes. I journaled, talked to my husband, and called friends as well. I was learning the power of vulnerability. All of this was challenging, but I never expected all I would face very shortly.

About eight months into my journey in the membership community, my very best friend was diagnosed with stage 4 pancreatic cancer.

She was in the emergency room, so I went to see her. She texted me telling me to identify myself as her daughter. They were still very selective about who was admitted because of COVID. She asked me to be strong for her before I left. I turned to her while fighting back tears and promised her that I would always be there for her, even if I cried. I kissed her forehead and told her I loved her. She said she loved me too. When I got home, just inside the door, I put my back against the wall and slid to the floor. I was hit with anguish and disbelief. My husband had gone shopping. He found me still on the floor when he got home and sat down with me. "They say it's cancer," was the only thing I could muster. No words were spoken. He simply sat beside me.

This is where the work really became real, and I got serious about self-care. I knew I had to do it to be there for her. I was initially motivated to do something important because of what I wanted to accomplish for someone else. I had made up my mind that there was no way I was going to let down someone who had always been there for me. She stood by my side, even in the worst of times. I started establishing limits and making decisions that were significant to me. It wasn't easy, and I often did it with shaking hands. I resisted urges to apologize despite feeling guilty. I would ask myself if I had done anything wrong. If the reply was negative, I would maintain my boundaries despite the discomfort. I began to allow people to have their own thoughts about my choices.

We had a grief and trauma specialist among the administration. She was one of the coaches. She attended a Zoom meeting in our group not long before my best friend was diagnosed and gave a lecture on grief. From the first time I heard her speak, I loved her. Being with her made me feel so relaxed and at ease. That day, she said something that I have remembered throughout my journey. "The experiencer defines the significance of the loss," she said. Nobody else has the right to judge the importance of the loss for you or how you should or shouldn't feel. From the time I made the decision to help my best friend's partner take care of her, I had her as my grief coach right by my side. I began meeting her once a week, and during some of my worst days, she sat with me and listened to me. She is one of the kindest, most understanding, patient, and composed people I have ever interacted with.

My grief coach told me I was resilient because of my experience as a carer. At first, I didn't believe her. I made the best effort I could, given everything I had to deal with, though. I took the good with the bad, the happy with the sad, and everything in between. We were all aware that it would happen eventually; we just didn't know when. After chemotherapy failed, she decided to simply live out her days. I had three 12-hour shifts at work, and the other four days of the week I spent trying to help her and her partner. I spent the night a lot and just spent time with her, taking her out for drives to do what she wanted and to eat where she wanted. When things started to get worse, they got worse quickly. It became more difficult for me to leave but also more difficult to return, the sicker she became. I experienced a great deal of mixed emotions. I wanted her suffering to end, but I also wanted her to stay. Even though I knew it was impossible, I still wanted her to improve in some way.

Things got hard, but I did not quit. About four hours before she passed away, I left. All I knew was that I had to leave. It was like God was telling me I had done all I could, and my work there was done. Leaving that day was one of the hardest days of my life. When I left, I knew I wouldn't see her again. When I was driving home, I was feeling emotionally numb, but I couldn't help but think back on what I had said to her before I left. She had a couple of tears in her eyes when I said goodbye. Was it a coincidence? No, I don't think so. I'll always believe she heard me.

People who read my posts, from coaches and counsellors to members of the membership community, were moved by my story. I was told that people's faith in people was restored by our story and how much my best friend and I loved one another. She was a beautiful person, and I miss her every day. She truly brought light into my life.

I discovered through the membership community how crucial it is to accept all emotions and that there are no good or bad emotions. It's important to experience every emotion, even the unpleasant ones. Through my experience providing care, I was learning how to put this into practice.

On October 4, 2021, my best friend would pass away in the wee hours. When she passed away, grief hit me hard. Both the winter and the holidays were challenging. I relied heavily on my network of allies. We considered each other family, as she was like a second mom to me. She always believed in me, even when I didn't believe in myself. She saw me beneath it all. She recognised the real me in me and had faith in my future. She frequently advised me to write a book because I have such a beautiful writing style, and yet here I am writing this chapter.

Early in the spring, I started to feel somewhat better, and I was looking forward to the warmer weather and getting out in my garden. Just six months after the death of my best friend, just as I was starting to feel a little better, my uncle passed away from a heart attack. Emotionally, I went numb. All the crying I was doing had suddenly come to a stop. So, here I was once more attempting to be present with myself and my feelings. I eventually did start crying. Growing up, my dad was absent in my life and I admired my uncle a lot. He was a good man. Not long after this loss, I realised that I was pushing myself too hard and got sick as a result.

At this point, I chose to accept a very kind offer from a coach in the membership group I was a part of. She needed clients for her trauma program while it was in progress, and I was in a position where I needed a lot of support. She is a wonderful, kind, caring, and generous person. I admire her greatly and am grateful for her. She has been incredibly helpful to me in my somatic and inner child work. Working with her has given me some pretty profound experiences.

I had a disagreement with a close friend a few months after the death of my uncle. She ended up deciding to no longer talk to me. I was once more overcome by intense agony. This loss was unlike any other I had ever experienced. Through my experience as a carer, she became my closet friend. I'll always be appreciative of everything she did for me. A lonely journey would have been even more lonely if not for her friendship. She still strikes me as a good person who is going through a difficult time, in my opinion. I do and will always care about her. Having said that, it is extremely difficult to grieve for someone who is still alive. She did not cooperate, despite my best efforts to reconnect. She ignored my repeated attempts to contact her. I, therefore, took the only action I could. I let her make her choice. I miss her, but part of loving someone is letting them go when they want to go.

I was a complete emotional wreck at this point. I experienced intense guilt, shame, and heartbreak, as well as intense anger, confusion, sadness, and anxiety. I also experienced loneliness, compassion, betrayal, and other emotions. I found it difficult to eat and sleep because of my overwhelming feelings. I was struggling mightily to complete the smallest tasks and was hardly functioning at all.

My physical health also started to deteriorate. I hardly had enough stamina to make it around the block without feeling worn out. I decided to visit my nurse practitioner and do something I had never done before. I requested time off work. I was aware that I was not okay and that it would not be beneficial to keep pushing myself. I realised that my self-awareness had probably saved me.

I ultimately took a total of about six weeks off. At first, I did not want to deal with or sit with the pain. Through social media scrolling and binge-watching TV shows, I discovered ways to avoid but I finally concluded that I had to stop running. Every morning, I took a cup of coffee and a journal outside to my patio. I focused on feeling each emotion as it came up and sitting with it. Many days seemed to go on forever. I was a mess from all the emotions I was experiencing. Again, my grief coach emphasized my resilience, but I still felt defeated.

I often ponder why some friendships endure while others do not. What I know does last, though, is the pain when they are gone. We will all experience grief at some point. As long as there is love, there will be grief. Even if the grief is for someone who is still living, it's still a beautiful thing to have loved. I have grieved for a few that are still living while on this journey. I've mastered the ability to experience both love and grief. I cherish the memories and am grateful for the lessons learned.

Having said that, I've recently experienced some very moving feelings of gratitude. I have experienced powerful moments that made me cry. I became aware of how much I was taking for granted as a result of all the sorrow and heartache and as a result of witnessing a sick person grieve the life they once knew. Grief alters you. It alters your perspective on the world and serves as a reminder of how precious every day spent with those you love is. Grief forced me to reconsider a lot of things. We only get just one time around.

I'm grateful for the profound life lessons that grief has given me. I am not saying I am happy for the suffering and hardship, the pain, or the losses. What I am saying is that I have gratitude for what the hard times have taught me and how I have grown as a person. I have learned how precious life is and how quickly things can change. With the people I love, I discovered how to be mindful and present. I discovered how to react quickly and calmly in times of need. I developed my grounding. I learned patience. I learned how to show up for myself when things were tough. I learned radical acceptance, letting go of what I could not control and focusing more on what I could. I learned how valuable communication is. I learned what real love is and what it looks like. I acquired the ability to let go. I learned to set boundaries. I learned to own my truth, regardless of what others thought. I learned that just because someone says or thinks something about me doesn't make it true. Even though I didn't agree, I started to sit and listen to other people's differing points of view and opinions. I started to ponder more ideas, widen my horizons, and get a better sense of the big picture. I started looking for things to fill my cup and my heart. I discovered that my importance is equal to that of others. To discover my worth, I learned to look within. I finally started to see the truth as I gradually started to overcome all the shame I had been carrying for such a long time.

I was also aware that I had attachment wounds and trauma to deal with. I am also aware that, as a result of this, I have injured other people. With the assistance the wonderful coaches in my life, I have learned how to examine my wounds, trauma, and patterns. I developed the ability to be compassionate towards every aspect of myself, even the parts that are in pain. The extent to which this aided in my healing astounded me. I developed the ability to take accountability for my behavior and make intentional change. Along with that, I had to be brave and to let those guiding me into my world. Even with trembling hands, I had to be totally honest with them.

After hitting rock bottom, I grew to love myself despite the suffering. It was empowering to learn that all this time, I was my hero.

Gratitude is incredibly potent and transformative. True gratitude does not preclude, however, experiencing sadness or pain. Gratitude does not cover up or cancel out any other emotion or experience. It can coexist with other emotions at the same time. More than one emotion can exist together. I am incredibly grateful for each person I lost and their presence in my life. At the same time, I can also feel sadness and grief.

By no means am I claiming that all grief involves gratitude, particularly when there has been suffering or abuse. I do understand there are more serious situations. I have had acquaintances that I would prefer to forget. I find it more beneficial to be grateful that I am no longer in that circumstance and grateful for my life. Each person's experience is their own.

Without my support network, I'm not sure where I would be. We aren't designed to do this alone because we are all hardwired for connection. Studies have demonstrated the advantages of learning and developing in a social context. I think my membership group has been a huge help to me in this area. This is where I met others who were travelling a similar path to recovery, and I was able to forge new international connections. My network of supporters only grew after that.

I don't know if I would have had the courage to open up and ask for help if my best friend hadn't responded to me so empathetically when I first opened up to her. I likely would have shut down again, leading to a whole different outcome. My best friend began this journey with me, and even though she is no longer here with us, I carry her with me always. She showed unconditional love. Without her, I don't know what I would have done.

Additionally, there is no shame in seeking out expert advice and assistance when necessary. It's amazing how much of a difference a single compassionate coach or counsellor can make in your life. However, I had to put in the effort. It truly is teamwork. I had to put in the work and make the changes in my life, and my coaches had to be invested, willing to listen and create a safe environment. Me investing in myself was also necessary. I had to pay attention and learn to rely on them for guidance. I am grateful because I get along so well with every coach I've worked with and have a close therapeutic relationship with my grief coach. She has helped me through a variety of grief scenarios.

She helped me cope with my anticipated grief. When that happens, time spent with a loved one is constrained. Though it's undoubtedly a form of grief, it's not always acknowledged as such. I am glad I had professional guidance through this. It provided me with time for myself to open up and share what I was experiencing that I otherwise would not have gotten. The fact that I made sure I had the assistance I required was also a form of self-care.

Additionally, my grief coach helped me cope with cumulative grief. This happens when losses happen in close succession quickly and there isn't enough time to process the previous loss. I went through cumulative grief after three significant losses within eight months. For me, depression started to resemble the symptoms of grief. For most of my life, I have battled depression intermittently. For me, it was hard to tell them apart. I had confidence in my grief coach because I knew she would let me know if she had any real concerns. The secret was ALWAYS being upfront and truthful with her.

And lastly, she helped me cope with an ambiguous loss. Another loss that is frequently not treated a form of grief in society is this one. This loss lacks a definite resolution. It leaves the person wondering if they should be grieving or holding out hope. When someone who is either still alive or whose condition is unknown is mourned, this occurs. I think this was the hardest for me and the one that mixed up my emotions the most. I also believed that I needed the most assistance during this.

Any kind of loss and grief can have a big effect. These are only a few I have listed. I no longer feel ashamed that I am supported by a team of mental health professionals. I can now clearly see how each of them has, in their unique way, significantly impacted my life. I will always hold a special place in my heart for each of them.

My experience with grief has taught me that it cannot be fixed and does not simply go away overnight. I am certain that I will always have it with me and I can learn to carry it. I can learn to ride the waves. Some days aren't so easy and I cry, some days are a little of both, but it's all okay. I've come to realise that practicing self-love is the only real way to deal with grief and learn to give it a space in your life. Acceptance is the greatest act of love we can give to those around us, and it also applies to our relationship with ourselves. There is no one we need love from more than ourselves when things are difficult and painful. Grief is the most courageous manifestation of self-love because it allows us to process all our feelings, regardless of how unpleasant, confusing, or messy they may be. No matter how challenging it becomes, we are showing up, accepting responsibility, and giving the message to ourselves the we matter and are worth it.

CHAPTER 12

How I was Catapulted into the Journey of Self-Love

Tanya Leach

"My favourite part of self-love is taking myself lightly and laughing at my silliness, enjoying myself and all I am and showing others, by my example, how to do that too."

As I lay in bed waiting, hardly daring to breathe, taking tiny, shallow breaths, I am anticipating the gunshot. Alert and perked up for even the slightest sound or movement. I eventually fall into a restless sleep as a result of exhaustion. I frequently wake up, and the bed next to me is still empty. I take in the silence all around me. I'm too terrified to go look. When dawn finally breaks on the following day, I rise and resume my normal daily activities. Making breakfast, cleaning the kitchen. As I get ready for work, I have trouble finding clothing that fits. My weight loss has been enormous. Although I can still breathe, I feel completely dead on the inside. I have become a shell of the person I once was. In this state, I'm a zombie.

Eight years later, I'm lying on a couch in a hypnotherapist's office. I've finally worked up the courage to end that traumatic relationship. I had left before; this wasn't the first time. Gosh, I had left so many times before, but that voice in my head had urged me to stay if I only made an effort to understand him a little better if I loved him more deeply if I worked harder, and if I wasn't so overly sensitive. The list kept going forever. But this time was unique. I didn't even let him know I was leaving this time. This time, while he was away, I packed my bags and left. I've not returned his calls this time. Somewhere, a strong survival instinct has arisen, and as a result, I am acting differently. My survival instinct has taken over.

The car radio blasts Gloria Gaynor's "I am what I am." My throat aches from straining to sing along loudly, and I feel as though my chest will collapse because these words are now so familiar to me. My anthem. And it marks the beginning of my path to self-love.

It has taken me 23 years to fully comprehend what it means to love oneself. There isn't a tiny box of self-love that you can open and put on to use as an invisible cloak. Respect, compassion, acceptance, lightness, forgiveness, kindness, awareness, and care for yourself are all components of self-love. It is a never-ending journey that is frequently tested, and I still encounter circumstances where I can see the gaps. I still encounter situations where I need to dig deep, become conscious of the things that react to me, and put in some effort.

I identified that I had patterns of:

Putting others' needs before my own.

Doing too much to feel valued (and not surprisingly, still not feeling valuable).

Being busy ALL the time to feel like I am good enough like I have to earn my value!

Not asking for help.

Feeling like everyone else does things way better than I can.

Feeling like I wouldn't be able to do something.

Feeling inferior to others.

People pleasing.

Perfectionism.

When confronted about his numerous affairs, my ex-partner claimed that I was overly sensitive, and insecure and that my jealousy was out of control. He also said that if it weren't for me, he wouldn't have any friends at all. I consequently began to think that those things were real. Therefore, my first lesson after ending the relationship was to understand that I was not in charge of his stuff and that it was okay for me to have felt those feelings given what he was doing. I was to blame for allowing him to treat me this way because I was unable to recognise my worth, but I was also responsible for it. I believed I deserved this kind of treatment because I wasn't trying hard enough, I wasn't loving enough, I was boring, and I wasn't pretty enough. The shocking state our relationship was in was entirely my fault. I decided to ignore his heavy drinking, his unresolved issues, and how the drugs he used made him more aggressive and depressed. I believed that if I performed better, I could magically and by myself turn everything around.

I now understand that his need for emotional regulation and affirmation through this kind of behaviour was motivated by his insecurities, low self-esteem, and profound unhappiness. It was in no way related to who I was or what I brought to the table. No one could satisfy his needs because he wasn't doing enough to satisfy them himself. I was always thinking about his happiness in this relationship and trying to satisfy his needs at the expense of my own. My requirements vanished. I withdrew from my loved ones and friends. I didn't want them to see how different I had become from who I once was. I wasn't prepared to accept the reality of the circumstance. I was hesitant to confront my fear of being by myself because I already felt inadequate. I thought that if I left, then I would be alone forever.

I've always had a natural empathy for other people and an understanding of their motivations. Today, it's what makes me a great coach and counsellor. However, it meant that everyone came to me to talk about their issues, to get support and guidance, and to be consoled. I suddenly realised that I had never reached out to others when I needed support after I woke up one morning. I handled issues and found solutions on my own. I never experienced such loneliness. Although I had wonderful family and friends, I had alienated everyone. I had kept to myself as I wallowed in my hell. I experienced failure. I was embarrassed by what I had allowed to occur and by my bad decisions. I felt unworthy. I carried around a sense of sadness and shame while still maintaining my composure in front of others and being there for anyone else who required a shoulder to cry on.

I eventually met my husband a few years later. He was very different from my ex-partner in many ways, but also very similar in many ways. He made me feel loved and beautiful. He inspired me to pursue my goals. His company was enjoyable. But he wasn't there for me emotionally. For the duration of our marriage, my husband took numerous business trips. He consulted me on this very infrequently. I just learned that he was heading to the UK for three weeks or that he would be leaving for Nigeria in two days. Without saying it out loud, I had the impression that I should be able to manage without any help from my family while managing a house, young children, and a full-time job. In addition to already having a full schedule, I had begun my studies for a degree in psychology. He assumed that everything would be in order in the house when he got home. It was, too. Always. Now that I look back, I see that I did this for myself. Another way to demonstrate my success as a wife, mother, and successful person. A significant portion of this role was probably based on my need to demonstrate to everyone that I was Superwoman and a portion was probably based on childhood conditioning that I hadn't let go of. I was unconsciously continuing the old pattern of putting everyone else's needs ahead of my own. I convinced myself that I had no other option. I told myself this was my role as a parent and wife. I ended up feeling exhausted, run-down, stretched too thin, angry, and resentful. My patience was limited. I lost my patience. I wanted to run away. I wanted to scream at everyone to leave me alone.

I persisted because of my amazing group of friends. I was able to get by for another week thanks to a Friday night gathering, a whine, and some female support. However, the holes were beginning to appear. My husband's connection to the family grew progressively worse. When he was at home, he spent a lot of time on his phone. He wasn't there emotionally or mentally. Given my past experiences, my biggest worry was that he might be having an affair. He had post-traumatic stress disorder from being in a war, and living in South Africa at the time increased his levels of aggression. He was doing this while I was doing more and more to cover for him. He felt unneeded and unwanted as a result, and I felt resentful and taken advantage of. We carried these feelings around without saying a word about them and were completely unaware of how they were festering underneath. We weren't in a good space.

I was starting to act differently thanks to my self-development work and the psychology I was studying. I saw the telltale signs of our unhappy marriage. I became aware of the separation and the space. I talked to him about the problems. I admitted to him that I thought he wasn't present or available. He dismissed it by pointing to work demands. After that, I suggested that he visit a psychologist, and he agreed. He stopped seeing her after three sessions, explaining that he didn't believe she was the right fit and that he would seek out someone else. He refused. He later admitted that he was unable to face the painful areas because she was getting too close to them.

About a year later, I learned that my husband had experienced an emotional affair several years prior. He had been laid off and felt that he was no longer needed at home or valued at work. She complimented him, gave him her full attention, and made him feel needed and wanted. A scenario out of a textbook. He suffered from low self-esteem due to bullying at school and other childhood events, which caused his need to prove himself, be validated, and provide entertainment to resurface. I had grown very independent due to his frequent travel and separation from the family. Overly independent. We were two single people living in the same house.

There were broken trust, tears, anger, pain, and sadness when I found out about the affair. I was finishing up my degree and applying to immigrate to Australia at the same time. Chasms formed from the cracks. There was a lot that needed to be resolved. My husband began seeing a fantastic psychologist when he realised that his marriage was going to end soon. After six months of intense therapy, he was finally able to start working through everything he needed to. I started using the information I already knew. I started making plans ahead of time for my needs. I set aside time for both my family and my friends. I had empathy for both myself and other people. I made time in the morning for exercise and cherished my lengthy beach strolls. The issues with my husband weren't mine. They weren't seen as things I was lacking in. He had work to do, and I had work to do too, as I realised. The breakdown in our marriage wasn't because of the affair. The affair was because we had disconnected, while we both struggled to feel like we were enough in the world. We just did it in different ways, using different resources.

Similar to a switch I concluded that I couldn't control anything, no matter how hard I tried. I was working myself to the bone trying to keep the house tidy, provide for the family, study, prepare delectable meals, be a mother and taxi driver for the kids, and do my best at work. I had to sit down and examine who I was. My degree and the vast knowledge I had gained from years of reading psychology books gave me the tools to turn inward and do the work. It was time to use the tools and skills I had, in my own life. I went to the counsellor. I got coaching. I let go of the need to be in total control, admitted the fears and lack of confidence that were motivating my actions, and started to lean into the procedure, the change, and the journey.

I began to consider the recurring pattern I was using at work. I had very little time or energy left for anyone or anything else, least of all myself, after taking on the tasks of three people. I used the logic that if I went above and beyond what was required of me at work, I would be seen as valuable, validated, and able to feel sufficient. I didn't have any restrictions at work. I didn't value myself highly enough to demand a salary that was commensurate with the heavy workload I carried. I started setting limits and giving the people and things that were and still are important to me a priority. I quit jobs that didn't compensate me fairly for the value I added (this has been a major challenge for me, but I've recently made significant progress in this area). I've overcome my fears and insecurities, and I value myself more than I ever have. I've accepted my innate talent for working with people in the counselling setting, and I love seeing my clients change every day. I am constantly inspired and motivated to learn new things and get better at what I do for my clients.

I turned the microscope on friendships and people that weren't healthy to have around me, friendships that I had kept just so that I could say I had loads of friends (because that meant I was loved, right? And if I was loved, it implied that at least some aspect of me was alright. I took stock of how far I had gone to feel important, loved, and like I belonged. In this situation, neither I nor anyone else was able to take advantage of me to my fullest potential. I began to firmly but gently object. I started to acknowledge my strengths. I considered my part in the breakdown of my marriage. I looked at how I was showing up or not showing up for myself and my loved ones. My self-talk was altered. I became conscious of my language and the unfavourable mental spirals that I was engaging in. I started keeping the promises I made to myself. I started stepping out of situations and looking at them from an observer's perspective. Sometimes, I didn't like what I saw. I, therefore, started actively choosing each day who I wanted to be and how I wanted to present myself to the world. Then, at the end of the day, just before going to bed, I evaluated the day to see if I had been the kind of person I wanted to be, and if not, I considered how I could change. I overcame my reluctance to trust and decided that if I wanted to stay in my marriage, I had to give it everything I had. I began to consider the emotions that I experienced when someone said or did something that caused me to feel offended, rejected, angry, or depressed. The areas of me that were bleeding began to heal little by little. I began living my life intentionally, and as a result, I began to love both myself and my life a little bit more every day.

I now feel completely at ease with who I am. I am conscious of who I am being each day and I strive to be my best self in every moment. I don't always get it right and when I don't, I speak to myself with compassion and kindness. I eat healthy meals and keep active because my health is important to me and to the longevity good health will provide me with so that I can have oodles of time with my family. I unfollow people to who I find I compare myself. When I do find myself comparing, I remind myself that this is my journey and each person's journey looks different. My fingerprints remind me that I am unique and therefore my life journey is unique too and it won't look like anyone else's. I meditate and practise stillness to check in with myself. I invite all my feelings to have a space in my body and process them with love, acceptance, and gentleness. I have forgiven myself for my mistakes, for my harshness and for when I have hurt someone. I recognise and celebrate my wins. I've let go of perfectionism – phew, this one put up a fight I can tell you! My favourite part of self-love is taking myself lightly and laughing at my silliness, enjoying myself and all I am and showing others, by my example, how to do that too.

I regularly think of the legacy I want to leave behind and what I would like that to be like, what I hope others would say of me when I have departed this world. While this may sound morbid, it's a wonderful way to ensure I live up to those values each day.

As I continue on this path of self-love, the peace, tranquilly, and lightness I experience every day is truly amazing. To be able to give my best in every circumstance, I support myself and consciously invite people and events into my life. Every morning, I look forward to what the day will bring because I know I can handle it. I accept myself exactly as I am, flaws and all, right now. I don't need to do anything to be worthwhile. I can change who I am to improve my interactions with others and myself, but I am already incomparably valuable. I invite you to embark on this journey because the benefits will be well worth it.

CHAPTER 13

From Fear to Love to Living My Dreams!

Shaima Alabbasi

"Self-love is not a destination but an ongoing journey of self-discovery, acceptance, and growth. It is a choice I make every day, a commitment to honor and cherish the incredible being that I am."

The wake-up call

I woke up to the familiar cry of my 16-month-old baby in the middle of the night. As I changed his diaper and prepared his bottle, I felt a heaviness in my heart, a constant companion that had plagued me for a while, an emptiness that I couldn't ignore any longer.

Since the Covid restrictions had started, I began reflecting on how my life was. I was happy being a stay-at-home mother of two at the time, but I felt the need for a change and didn't know what to do or how.

Little did I know that it was the absence of self-love.

But on that night, something within me shifted. A tiny spark of hope flickered amidst the darkness. I realized that if I wanted to find happiness and fulfillment, I needed to do something about it. It was time to rewrite the narrative that played on an endless loop in my mind.

That shift didn't just happen overnight. I was then mourning the death of my cousin, who was my closest childhood friend, to cancer.

His passing deeply affected my family and the shock and grief of losing someone so young and close served as a wake-up call for me.

After grieving for a while as well as going into covid lockdown, I contemplated this "new world", and came to the profound realisation that life is short and precious.

And that caused my mind to race with so many thoughts.

I'm unsure of when my time on this planet will come to an end.

I don't want my life to end with sadness, regret, or disappointment!

So, I asked myself: When will I take action on towards achieving my dreams?

I've quit my full-time job to take care of my family, putting off any desires to pursue my ambitions. This being due to my belief that being a mother is the highest achievement there is. Yet, I still had a part of me that needed fulfillment, and wondered when this wait was going to end.

Practicing my dream of becoming a trainer and a public speaker didn't seem feasible back then because I knew it wouldn't be easy with two children under the age of six, as they constantly need someone to watch them.

Being in lockdown made me realize that I can develop my skillset and expand my knowledge online while I take care of my kids, and in doing this, I will be well prepared to start practicing when they are old enough.

That's when I decided to take my dream seriously. I did some research and I found out that coaching, training, and public speaking have so much in common. So, I signed up with a coaching school in Australia, which was my first step towards self-love!

Old beliefs

For so many years, I assumed that "learning to love yourself" came naturally!

How is it possible for someone to hate themself?

I had no idea that self-love went deeper than having a good time with friends, enjoying a hobby, or even just eating well and exercising.

My parents' divorce, when I was a young child, had a significant negative impact on my emotional health, which was a major contributor to my difficulties, even though it didn't show on the surface. I grew up with a victim mentality and a genuine belief that I was broken just because I don't live in a typical family, let alone the complications, confusion or drama that result from it.

I was the "good girl" who excels in school and worked extremely hard in everything I did because somehow, I learned as a young child that happiness comes from receiving external validation and approval from others. For this reason, for many years, I fed my self-worth and confidence by receiving praise and admiration from others.

I placed such a high value on other people's approval that I would become upset and sad if I learned that they weren't pleased with me. As a result, I would go to great lengths to make things right, even if it was at my own cost, which made it easier for some people to emotionally manipulate me.

This sometimes made the journey lonely and filled me with uncertainty, and I had no idea how to get around it. I was unsure of how to make it better.

I was unaware that this was a flawed assumption until I discovered how to love myself through learning tools and strategies to dig deep in the human psyche and change it for the better! And that is one of the greatest gifts I have ever discovered and consider a great blessing.

My ambitious self

Since I started my coaching studies, I unleashed a part of me that was hibernating for a long time! I was working on something that was mine, and mine alone: my personal development. And what made it sweeter was the fact that everything I was doing and learning was going to prepare me to help others later on as well and fill the void I felt at the same time.

As Covid restrictions were still in effect worldwide, I observed people complaining about the boredom of staying at home. I had the exact opposite experience. Thanks to modern technology, which allowed me to take part in a global community and an Australian institute, in the comfort of my home in Bahrain. I had a blast learning and developing as a person and a coach with a positive, supportive and loving community.

I had to participate in several live online training sessions that ran six hours each day for a few days a week. I had to get up at 2:45 am to attend these events because I live on the opposite side of the planet.

The only time I was able to take a power nap was during lunch breaks when people were eating!

I'm incredibly grateful to my mother for watching my kids while I stayed at her place during the lockdown. This allowed me to rest for a few hours after a day of training before I resumed my motherhood responsibilities.

Reflecting back on how I did my studies, I doubt that I would have chosen those 'crazy timings' to attend live training if I had the option. I can see that it was actually the ideal setup for me because I learned—and this lesson didn't hit me until much later—that the only time I could attend a lengthy training was while my kids were asleep.

That's how I was able to accomplish a lot of other things, like coaching my private clients and doing my live coaching assessments. My self-worth grew as I took time off for self-development as well as sharing the knowledge I acquired by coaching others.

Applying a lesson from the German philosopher Friedrich Nietzsche: "He who has a "why" to live for can bear almost any "how", I looked for times when I could multitask and use that time to finish some studying. So, while driving or doing the dishes, I would listen to a recorded lesson. I even purchased specialized waterproof speakers, in order to listen while taking a shower! Yes, I was that dedicated, especially considering that I had a large number of lessons to watch for my certification assessment.

My ambitious, dedicated, goal-oriented self was on a role!

I didn't realize how much I missed that side of me until I started to invest in professional development, and now I don't want to let go!

With the joy and excitement that came with this experience, for the first time in my life, I was the source of my own pride and confidence as I saw that I was smart and strong. I could get things done, face and manage challenges in addition to being a full-time mother!

That in itself was a huge accomplishment and a big leap in my journey to loving myself!

Chaos!

But the journey of self-love was not without its challenges.

I found out I was pregnant with my third child while I was preparing for the highest level of training I could ever participate in, which was all about facilitation.

I was on the verge of quitting a few days before the training started, but then I thought, I've signed up and did prepare, I'll do it. And during the training itself, on day four, I remember getting so exhausted that I considered quitting again. Waking up at 1:45 am and staying up for more than 6 hours, with two kids while in my first trimester, plus presenting and getting stretched every day, was so intense!

Then again, I thought, I've come this far, just one more day to go, let me get it done, I don't know if I'll get the opportunity to do it in the future.

I'm so glad I continued because that training stretched me so much and made me the speaker and trainer I am today!

Despite the challenge of staying up for crazy hours, with nausea almost the whole time, I found some relief thanks to my husband's support. We had prearranged that he would look after our children, allowing me to recover for a few hours post-training. This assistance was invaluable, and I am eternally thankful for having such a supportive spouse.

A significant lesson I learned from that training was the importance of embracing the chaos that surrounds me. Previously, I tended to seek order and control, relying on a clear structure and outline, which made "training" easier as I could rely on prepared content. I used to feel anxious about audience questions because I didn't know what to expect or how to respond in the moment. This challenge also extended to my everyday life. However, since I began accepting my shortcomings and actively working on improving my skillset, this mindset has shifted, and I started to go with the flow and enjoy the ride as anxiety was replaced with a sense of fun and adventure.

Facilitation is a whole other game! It's all about letting go of structure, involving the audience and making it an enjoyable, unpredictable, fun experience for everyone!

It taught me to face my fears, as it wouldn't kill me to accept my imperfection because I'm simply human. I also learnt to let go of the need for structure and control, and enjoying the fun of taking myself lightly, which helped me present speeches and trainings with more ease and flow.

Beyond delivering to an audience, that lesson in particular helped me to return to my studies and coaching after my maternity break.

It wasn't easy at the beginning; in fact, I had planned to delay my return to coaching and studying until my baby turned six-months. As doubts crept into my mind from time to time, threatening to undo all the progress I had made, it was in those moments that I turned to my support system—supportive friends, coaching colleagues whom I considered as family, and mentors, who believed in me when I couldn't believe in myself. They reminded me of my strength and resilience, helping me find the courage to carry on.

Then I remembered that I can "embrace the chaos", and that I can use my situation as an opportunity to learn and grow, so I resumed my studies when my baby was just three months old.

Surprisingly, what I assumed might be viewed as unprofessional by my clients was met with respect and admiration. I was coaching while nursing my baby or rocking her to sleep. Some clients even expressed gratitude for my dedication, explaining that my ability to balance my personal life with my professional commitments demonstrated how to continue pursuing their passions despite facing obstacles.

Inner work

As my knowledge deepened in human behavior, I saw how I had been my own worst critic my whole life! Every step I took, every decision I made, was met with a flood of self-doubt and self-criticism. I compared myself to others, always finding myself lacking. It seemed that no matter how hard I tried, I couldn't measure up to the idealized versions of success and perfection that I held in my mind.

I began acknowledging the negative self-talk that had held me back for so long. Day by day, I made a conscious effort to replace self-criticism with self-compassion. With practice and patience, I broke free from my constant need for control and perfectionism by gently reminding myself that I was only human, flawed but also beautiful in my imperfections.

Instead of seeking external validation, and feeling frustrated when I couldn't get any, I celebrated my small victories, no matter how small they seemed. Each time I stumbled, I picked myself up with kindness and forgiveness, refusing to let setbacks define my worth. That came a long way in the progression of my day-to-day tasks with kids and household responsibilities.

To nourish my soul, I practiced my religion, Islam, which is – and always has been – a part of my daily life. I pray five times a day, I read the Qura'an (the Holy Muslim's book) and I practice the religion's teachings that regulates my whole life. Speculating to Allah (God), asking him for strength and guidance is one important practice, when I feel so vulnerable and lonely, knowing that He watches over me and will help and guide me through my journey.

Gratitude and being thankful for what I have is another important Islamic practice. Focusing on what is there instead of what is missing, shifts my mood and defeats any negative thoughts. It helps me focus on what matters and to find good in everything.

I know mothers will agree when I say that a mother can't take breaks easily, with or without a job! Nevertheless, knowing how important self-care is, I dedicated a few hours a week to going out with friends to recharge my energy. If that was difficult, I would spend half an hour watching a comedy show or even ten minutes enjoying a cold drink or a piece of chocolate and that would do the trick! I just needed to be aware to tell myself that it was my "me time", a reward for my efforts that day or week. That served as a mental break from my daily stress.

When it comes to my physical needs, I learned to listen to my body. I took breaks to lay down whenever I got a chance if I felt tired and asked for help when needed. That is the opposite of what I used to do; pushing through the pain to get the task done without asking for help as I thought it meant that I was inadequate.

As my emotional well-being is a vital part of my personal needs, I surrounded myself with positive influences and got away from negative people or even conversations that no longer served me. I learnt how to say no when I recognized something that would affect my emotions negatively.

This whole package of inner work, put together, is how I continue to love and take care of myself.

The Truth

Ironically, many people look to others or "things" to make them feel good, and I was one of them for almost all of my life.

Only after receiving proper training and education in human behavior, did I realise that it is an inside job, as "self-love" implies.

It doesn't matter what happened to you in your childhood, nor your current circumstances.

I learned the truth of self-love as I progressed deeper into my studies, and by applying my new learnings and managing different challenges as they came along. With each passing day, I felt a shift within me. The heaviness in my heart began to lift, replaced by a sense of lightness and freedom. I started to see myself through a different lens—a lens of compassion and acceptance. The more I loved myself, the more love I had to give to others. And in doing so, I discovered that self-love is the fuel one needs to progress and develop in life.

I realized that the relationship we have with ourselves is important for us to be able to process and release the past, as well as manage and live with our current life, and then we can all achieve and enjoy this simple yet profound truth, but only if we so choose.

All it takes is a willingness to leave our comfort zones, be open to new concepts that were not taught to us growing up, have the willingness to make the necessary changes, with patience and then watch how the changes take place.

After a while of participating, picking up new ideas, and putting them into practice, I realised that one of the self-empowerment foundations I needed to lay, was accepting responsibility for my outcomes. I don't want to blame anything or anyone for where I am or how my life might develop.

With the ability to do that, I also learned that having a positive relationship with myself—which is the foundation of self-love—relies primarily on one thing—and one thing alone—my self-talk!

According to Jim Kwik, self-talk functions like an operating system for our brain, dictating our actions. The brain doesn't differentiate between true or false, realistic or unrealistic, planned or unplanned, beneficial or detrimental, conscious or subconscious thoughts. It lacks filters, judgments, and reasoning; it merely listens to our self-talk and responds to it as if it were a command to be followed.

This is where the power and danger lie.

It's a double-edged sword because the language we choose influences our sub-conscious mind and, in turn, affects our brain's functions, influencing our decisions and life overall!

Self-Love

By integrating the understanding of self-talk and principles like taking action, consistency, and responsibility, I experienced a transformative shift in my life, which I expect to have a continuous effect until my last breath.

Reflecting on my past, I realize that I wasn't prepared for the challenges of motherhood. As my family grew, I faithfully embraced the conventional full-time mother role, only to find myself overwhelmed by stress, blame, resentment, and exhaustion.

But after making the mental shift, each time I faced a challenge with my kids or another "grown-up" issue and overcame it, I gave myself a pat on the back, smiled, and said, "Well done Shaima, you're doing great given the resources you have. You rock!"

As a result, I stopped whining about how difficult my day was and how I needed more support when my husband got home from work. Instead, I started to feel proud of myself and more motivated to get things done.

Although I don't blame him or try to win his sympathy, I do talk to him about my day.

I was already proud of myself; I don't need it from anyone else.

It would be a bonus if someone else complimented me, of course!

Awareness

Please understand that I'm not claiming to be a supermom or to carry the weight of the world on my shoulders.

Like everyone else, I am a normal human being with limited energy, 24 hours a day, and a ton of things to do.

And to this day, I still place a high value on excellence and "doing the right thing." The difference is that I now do it with a different level of awareness and self-love in mind.

I persevered to get to where I am now without going crazy by being mindful of my needs, wants, desires, and goals as well as by aiming for success and excellence.

Now I understand myself more. I know my limits, and I don't push myself beyond those limits.

I've also learned to be kind to myself and not judge myself when I'm too tired or pressed for time to complete a task.

In times of fatigue, I take breaks.

When I need assistance or support, I ask for it.

I decline invitations to events, activities, or even conversations that don't benefit me or come in the way of my progress.

Whatever happens and no matter what anyone says, as long as I'm doing the best I can, I'm good.

All of those self-love techniques made me gain the awareness that I am enough and that others will treat me with the respect and consideration that I deserve only when I recognise my value and have unyielding boundaries. I only realised this after putting them into practice.

Living the Dream

Through my journey, I learned that every life experience, no matter how tough or painful, prepares us for what lies ahead. This aligns with the teachings of the Qur'an: "But you may hate a thing although it is good for you, and may love a thing although it is bad for you. Allah (God) knows, and you do not." (2:216)

I have no doubt that I wouldn't have come this far if it wasn't for every single experience I had since I was a child.

I now serve as a confidence coach for mothers, guiding them to heal their internal wounds and boost their self-esteem through personal and group coaching, workshops, and a podcast. I also teach people how to present with confidence, overcome self-doubt and imposter syndrome, and deliver their message effortlessly.

I can't claim that I am living 'The Dream.' The only thing I know for sure is that I've embarked on the journey towards self-love, which, in my opinion, is the real dream.

The notion of 'the perfect life' or 'the dream life' is a deceptive illusion that can prevent us from following our true desires. Chasing an improbable goal can be demotivating because it feels unreachable. Alternatively, if one truly believes in achieving the 'perfect life,' they may end up working to the point of breakdown, constantly unsatisfied, unable to enjoy the present, and continuously craving more without appreciating their blessings.

Choosing such a life can be incredibly exhausting.

In my view, the ideal approach is to strive for self-improvement while expressing gratitude for what we have and giving back to others. That's my definition of a dream life! It's about progress, not perfection. It's an ongoing process, a continuous journey.

As a Muslim, I deeply believe that life doesn't end with death. Instead, our earthly existence lays the foundation for our eternal afterlife. Consequently, our real 'happily ever after' is a choice, not a fairytale.

With the pursuit of a fulfilling life, I'm aware that my path will have challenges that will test me and make me stronger with every decision I make.

My real Dream is not here on earth!

It's up above!

I'm aiming beyond the stars!

Michelangelo's quote captures this perfectly: "The greatest danger for most of us is not that our aim is too high, and we miss it, but that it is too low, and we reach it.".

Lessons learnt

As I reflect on my personal journey of self-discovery and growth, I have come to a profound realization: self-love is the key that unlocks the door to true happiness and fulfillment. It has been a transformative process, one that required me to shed old beliefs and embrace a new way of thinking.

Self-Love

Through the ups and downs, the triumphs and setbacks, I have learned to be kinder to myself, to quiet the voices of self-doubt, and to replace them with words of encouragement and self-acceptance. I have discovered the power of journaling, as the written word became my sanctuary, allowing me to explore my deepest thoughts and emotions with honesty and vulnerability.

The support and love from my community have been instrumental in my journey. Surrounded by like-minded souls who uplift and inspire, I have found strength in their belief in me. And when the road became challenging, I asked Allah (God) for strength and sought the guidance of professionals, understanding that seeking help is an act of courage, not weakness.

Taking time for myself has become a non-negotiable part of my routine. It is during those moments of solitude that I reconnect with my essence and rediscover the joy and wonder that resides within me.

I have come to understand that perfection is an illusion, and that celebrating even the smallest wins is crucial. Each step forward, no matter how small, takes me closer to the person I aspire to be. And in each moment, I practice gratitude for the gifts my Creator has filled my life with and the blessings and lessons that have shaped me.

Living in the present has become my mantra, releasing the worries of the future, and embracing the beauty of the now. It is in this state of mindful presence that I find peace and satisfaction, allowing life to unfold with its own rhythm and flow.

And so, as my story reaches its conclusion, I realize that self-love is not a destination but an ongoing journey—a journey of self-discovery, acceptance, and growth. It is a choice I make every day, a commitment to honor and cherish the incredible being that I am.

With each passing day, I am reminded that I am deserving of love, happiness, and all the wonderful things life has to offer. I am my own greatest ally, my own source of strength. And as I embrace this newfound self-love, I step into the world with confidence, knowing that I am enough, worthy, and capable of creating a life filled with love and purpose.

CHAPTER 14

What is Self-Love, To Put It Down To A Single Sentence?

Katherine Jackat

"Self-Love is the highest frequency."

What does self-love mean to a person who spent their childhood surrounded by self-destructive habits and parents who seemed to have little to no affection for one another? When self-love isn't preached or demonstrated, how does one learn to take care of themselves with it?

Perhaps it's to spend every day alone in the shed drinking beer because you've had a hard day at work and that's what you deserve. Perhaps the best way to lose weight is to eat cheesecake, M&Ms, and chocolate freckles for breakfast every day. Or is smoking a few cigarettes when I'm feeling stressed or anxious considered "self-care"? To give myself a nicotine dose to feel calm so I could recognise how I was feeling. Perhaps it's to exert control over those around me so that I can have control over my uncontrollable life.

Bitterness has developed between the parents and children as a result of their upbringing in this environment with parents who struggle internally. Family disconnection and abusive communication Making their children believe they are burdens or unlovable is the ultimate atmosphere they can create. This has aided in the development of some of my struggles, including self-destructive behaviours, toxic behaviour towards others, and a pessimistic outlook on life.

My journey towards self-love, self-care, self-respect, or anything else related to "self" has been a major emotional rollercoaster, a major mood swing, and a major pain in the behind. Take a dive with me.

All through high school, it was intense and overwhelming. I once thought, "How on earth am I going to be enough at school when I can never be enough at home?" In school, I had many failures. Not because I'm stupid, but rather because I didn't give a damn. I didn't give a damn about my education or what it was 'preparing' me for. At this time, I couldn't have cared less about how it would impact me but, damn, was I lying to myself. I really did care, and I really felt like a failure. What a cycle to be in.

Maybe the additional instruction, tutoring, or even a $12,000 computer programme would help me concentrate and learn. Maybe I won't be such a failure at everything after all. To be clear, it did indeed help. I now have a lot more faith in my ability to learn and in myself. After a couple of years, my success began. Perhaps it's because I've grown to care. It was more addicting to see my parents proud or loving than to see them full of disappointment. I still take great pride in the A++ I received for my creative writing and water safety projects in my 8th-grade sports class. Or when I had to read a book in ninth grade, I chose a character (who wasn't the main character) and wrote a 'spin-off' chapter about their life. I didn't read the book; fuck, I didn't even get through the first chapter; however, I was able to write my chapter and get an A. I've said it before, I'm not stupid; I just didn't care.

But this was short-lived. Life at home and school became challenging, and friendships failed to endure.

Now that I'm older, I can see that my parents wanted the best for me; they exerted every physical effort to aid in my academic improvement. But fuck, I still felt like I lacked sufficient self-worth.

I had the impression that nothing in my life was under my control. I had a parent figure who would constantly remind me that their home was only a stopgap and that I might end up on the streets if they decided I was no longer wanted. Making plans with friends for the evening without suffering consequences was out of my control. I wasn't allowed to do anything on the weekend until all the chores were done. Ironically, I never cleaned nor properly completed my chores. On occasion, when I was asked to help in the kitchen with dinner preparation, I would peel a potato or even a carrot somehow incorrectly. Then, out of nowhere, I had enraged this parent figure to the point where I would receive abusive yells.

My first experience with a blade on my skin occurred when I was 14 years old. I failed yet another class, I was embarrassed and upset with myself. Although I had previously considered it, I had never actually considered doing it. I pushed with this. It turned out to be a getaway. I thought I was in charge. When I did this, all of the anger, frustration, and sadness would subside. Never deep or extreme, just enough to draw a little blood and cause an endorphin rush. I only harmed myself occasionally. Just when I needed a release or when life became too much.

I recall the day my mother first noticed them. It was as we prepared to drive to her friend's house, she complimented me on how lovely I looked in my dress. Oh, gosh, the guilt was unbearable. I asked to leave halfway through to go to my friend's house because I was feeling overwhelmed with anxiety, shame, and embarrassment. For the first time, I was able to talk openly about this problem, and I will always be grateful that I did. My very first self-love gesture

It wasn't long after that incident, that I was taken to the doctor. Mum pleaded with me to be more honest. I declined and claimed to be fine. She still accepted me, seated me next to my doctor, and the room was silent. Mum was uncomfortable and speechless. She and I both had to have found this uncomfortable, I knew. Then the query arose: "So, Katherine! What brought you in here today?" he exclaimed. Mum watches to see if I respond, but I only shrug.I can still recall feeling so uneasy that all I wanted to do was go home and sit in my room." Separate myself from my surroundings. Harm. "She's been a bit of a bitch lately, and I think she needs to open up." Says, Mum. My mouth fell open, and my doctor gave me a worried look.

I'm now by myself with him as Mum gets up to leave. This was the second occasion when I was forced to talk to speak up. Before I knew it, I had another appointment scheduled. The only distinction was that this call was made via Skype. I recall it so vividly: it was a tiny, dim room hidden in the medical centre's back. It had a nice computer and was set up with a glass of water for me, so I'm sure it was a storage room. The nurse was gracious; she showed me how to use the computer and instructed me to connect when I was ready. Because I didn't want to be kept here any longer, I connected almost immediately. The appointment started when two doctors appeared on the screen. I can still picture myself in the camera and thinking, "How disgusting." They might not notice me and ask too many questions if I lean to the side, just out of view. Is that how I really look?

I felt terrible for putting my mother through this. This is just one more stress she doesn't need given how chaotic her home life already is. All of it is my fault. I 'yessed' and 'ahh-huhhed' my answers, not really thinking too much about the questions. When it was over, they promised to connect me with the "wonderful" teen psychologist who lived close to where I lived. I thanked them, grinned awkwardly, and ended the call.

I soon began seeing my new psychologist. It was okay; every Thursday, I got a half-day just to sit and talk. What a fantastic way to finish school early! It wasn't all bad, but I did try to occupy too much of my appointment time with schoolwork or socialising with friends rather than things that were actually affecting me. I told her a little bit about my family and how I believed that my parents' marriage was under more strain now that I was here. I told her that because I didn't want to burden my parents, I stayed quiet and promised to do everything in my power to be the perfect young lady they could have asked for. I soon received a diagnosis of anxiety and the beginnings of depression.

Over the course of the following ten sessions, I discovered how to manage my anxiety and confront my depressing, unloving thoughts. It was beneficial. But I continued to harm myself. But learning how to help myself was the third time I experienced self-love. This was mainly self-acceptance and respect. I was made aware of how thoughtful and caring I am, and how challenging the idea of being a burden would enable me to get past my overwhelming sense that I am not doing enough.

I was done after those ten sessions were over. They asked me to return, but I refused because I knew the sessions wouldn't be free. I was aware of the financial strain on my parents and had no intention of adding to their troubles.

During my last few therapy sessions, I found myself in my first relationship. Then again, it wasn't a good one. To cut a long story short, I endured a lot of verbal abuse, manipulation, and control from both parties, but I persisted for almost 6 years. I was able to stop self-harming as a result of that relationship because my then-boyfriend threatened to leave if I didn't stop. Although it didn't really help, I do still feel grateful for that in a way. You see, even though I stopped physically hurting myself, I thought I still needed that control in some aspects of my life.

I changed my self-harm into a habit of not eating.

I won't say that I have an eating disorder because I haven't received a diagnosis, but I am fully aware that if I wanted to avoid gaining weight or lose some weight, I would avoid eating. I am well aware that I occasionally try to go two days without eating. But now I was in charge. These are choices I make. I choose to weigh myself every day and permit myself to eat more than one meal each day. I am in charge of myself.

I was in this relationship even though I knew we weren't a good match. I persisted in my belief that I needed this relationship to feel worthy, wanted, and sufficient. I also believed that this relationship, with all the arguments, misunderstandings, deceit, and frustration, was typical. It was the way I was raised. a love that is unhealthy. I won't go into detail, but what I perceived as love was a lot of disrespect, obsession, and control. I required a sense of selection and desire. I couldn't love myself unless he showed me that he loved me.

Although I wasn't aware of it at the time, this was another lesson in self-love. Not to be forced to eat, but to realise that when I eat sensibly, I can still come to love myself. I began to realise that food is fuel and that my body depends on it to survive and flourish.

While all of this was going on, my family was in danger of going without a home. After Mum was laid off, the time, until we were homeless, began to tick down.

It's very challenging for me to create this image for you as I sit here. My parents used to argue a lot at night. My mother is always whining about my father's drinking and smoking. Accusing him of squandering their money on things he should not be and failing to consider the family. She never really spoke about it until I asked. I mean, why wouldn't I? They're always fighting about it anyway.

I don't remember my parents being respectful or being kind to one another. I don't remember a time when a conversation about money wouldn't turn into disagreements. Months of bickering and rude remarks turned into years. Years turned into decades. But that's okay because this is love. This is normal. One alcoholic parent figure, and one who brings up the kids. One who blames the kids for everything, and one who blames the other parent. Kids, addictions, and financial stress—the marriage life Normal.

I was working by this time, and now I was eager to start to help pay bills, to which my mum declined every time. I watched her apply for hundreds of jobs, to then be knocked back by so many. 3 months left until the last of the extra repayments break even and the bank starts asking for payments to be met again.

How is it possible to learn to love oneself in a challenging and unloving environment? How can someone possibly love themselves when their home could be taken away?

Don't worry, though; this was more about learning to love oneself. Because of this, I now understand how crucial it is to have an emergency fund and be current on your bills. For my future self to be able to survive for a few months while I think about my next move. I suppose it qualifies as a "basic life skill," but how many people actually perform this for themselves?

My mother was soon able to advance quickly within the company after obtaining a temporary job. an extremely important position. We're protected.

I can still picture myself pausing while scrolling through Facebook to read a friend's network marketing post. I quickly entered the game and gave it everything I had. I was incredibly excited. I was so prepared for this potential new life. I considered all the money I could earn. I considered how I could eliminate my parents' financial stress by paying off their house. After that, they would be able to fall in love once more. I considered all the additional people I could assist and all the additional donations I could make. I even entertained the idea of actually owning my own home and felt happy about the fact that I wouldn't have to worry about being evicted at any time. I was ecstatic about all the potential!

This was the community that taught me the most self-love one could ever stumble upon, even though I've been in and out of networking over the years.

This particular group genuinely believed that life would never grant you what you desired if you lacked self-love, self-worth, or self-respect. If one did not have confidence in themselves or trust, dreams would never come true. There were endless possibilities for how to focus on yourself physically. More reading. Take daily walks. Be awake early. Consume more whole foods. Recognise your body's needs and heed them. If you feel overwhelmed, slow down. Take more baths (this I did, I turned into a routine for every Sunday – didn't last long though, as I was yelled at for using too much water).

As I tried to do all these physical things, my mental health gradually reverted to its state of loneliness and misery. I resumed cutting back on my eating, increased my napping, and stopped calling on friends. Maybe I was a failure after all.

Life is too difficult, here we go again. On some days, I consider my options for how to end my life. But I am aware that I am not suicidal.

There is a saying that states that you will never be happy if you don't work on your inner self. This might be what I was missing. Numerous people in my immediate vicinity had been discussing the value of having a life coach. I then made my second significant step towards seeking guidance, and in all honesty, they are correct. I gained a lot of self-knowledge and increased self-awareness about many of my struggles.

I continue to be grateful for my coaches because they were the ones who helped me shine a light on what, in my opinion, self-love is. It turns out to be quite a bit. Family time is now a time for solitude, healing and connecting. It's taking long drives while listening to music or meeting a friend for coffee. It's working on the rough unlovable side of myself. It involves identifying and addressing my pains and triggers. It involves letting myself breathe, slow down, and have faith in myself. Simply purchasing flowers or allowing myself to Overspend and not overthink money can qualify as this behaviour. It involves forgiving those who have wronged me and mending strained family ties. It's personal development, acceptance, kindness, and respect.

What is self-love, to put it in a single sentence?

Self-love is the highest act of all five love languages combined.

CHAPTER 15

The Goddess Within

Lisa Infante

> *"Self-love is not based on a single deed or behaviour. It's not a place to get to ("Yes, I've arrived at self-love and can cross that off my bucket list!"), but rather a mindset that supports yourself."*

"Who does she think she is walking around like that?"

"OMG, she thinks she's so much better than everyone else!"

"She's totally in love with herself—get over it!"

You might be familiar with these if you think back to your school days (hello, teenage angst and insecurity!). In the schoolyard, self-love, self-care, and anything else that suggested you held yourself in high regard were things to be ashamed of and avoided at all costs, as if being proud of and loving yourself implied that you were conceited or snobby and possibly a tall poppy that needed to be cut down. The phrase "in love with yourself" was associated with negative connotations, such as a lack of concern for other people's needs and a belief that one was superior to them. At worst, it suggested that the individual was a bitch. This was my experience in school, and now that I think about it, even at university and in my first full-time job!

I didn't get into the self-development business until I was in my thirties and had reached an "emotional rock bottom." I had been a fan for years, but the only reason I cared about it was for the motivational sayings I used as feel-good screensavers, or for the chance to post something on my Facebook wall to prove to myself that I was content (or, let's be honest, as a not-so-subtle way to let someone know they'd irritated me - yes, Frenemy, that passive-aggressive quote about strong women not caring about petty judgement WAS about you)!

Imagine my complete surprise when I read about self-love and learned that it was not a sign of narcissistic self-importance, but that the true act of loving yourself was a lovely process of gratitude, kindness, and patience. One that encourages you to love and support others more, while also feeling great about yourself! I was astounded!

To understand the powerful effects of self-love, you need to know what it looks like when there's an absence of it. Take a trip down memory lane with me.

In the traditional Italian culture I grew up in, both men and women proudly fulfilled a set of predetermined roles that had been handed down from the generations before them. The most intriguing thing to me was how women were content to follow men's leadership blindly while men were responsible for making important life decisions. This is not intended to start a discussion about gender or culture; rather, it is just my perspective as a young girl. Nobody seemed to give much thought to personal preferences; people appeared to live their lives largely in accordance with societal norms and expectations.

I learned as a child that I could be anything I wanted to be and that my opinion mattered. However, I perceived it through a cultural lens, which led me to believe that I had a duty to avoid offending anyone and to keep them happy. Regardless of whether it conflicted with my personal principles or beliefs, maintaining the peace was of the utmost importance. This belief became deeply ingrained in the way I would later present myself in romantic relationships and the way I allowed men to treat me after witnessing the shocking and painful breakdown of my parents' marriage when I was in my mid-teens.

At the tender age of 18, I met the boy of my dreams. On paper, he was everything I needed—or at least everything I "should" need—but my needs weren't met. He was a nice guy, and I was lucky to have him, so I stuck with him for seven years despite having a strong gut feeling that this relationship wasn't going well and wondering what the hell was wrong with me. Even though I wasn't happy and felt like an imposter. Because I didn't want to burden anyone with my insecurities and, to be honest, I didn't think I was good enough for him, I struggled for years to express what I needed from the relationship. The fact that we broke up should have served as a wake-up call for me to find my voice, but what fun it is to learn a lesson the hard way!

From that point on, I dated men who were either manipulative and controlling or emotionally aloof and selfish, which caused a brief pendulum swing. Because I had a deep-seated fear of being alone, I based my sense of self-worth on how well I was liked by others. After marrying the man of my dreams, I felt "complete" at last. But once more, the same thing occurred: people-pleasing, unmet needs, and resurfacing insecurities. Divorce was the end result. With the shame and social stigma that came with being a single mother, my self-love metre was at an all-time low.

I questioned everything about myself, including whether I had too many expectations, if my boundaries were too loose, and whether I ought to be more assertive or hold fewer opinions. I met Mr Narcissist, a man skilled in the art of gaslighting who would destroy what little self-esteem I still had when I was in this emotional seesaw state of being. There is simply no other way to put it… Threats, insecurity, and manipulation fueled our toxic and destructive relationship. The psychological and emotional trauma I went through filled me with anxiety, resulting in frequent panic attacks and a situational depression diagnosis. I was a lost shell of the person I once was. I despised the person I had become and was appalled by the example I was giving my son. Knowing that I had allowed this to happen because I didn't value myself enough was a bitter pill to swallow. I was responsible for destroying myself by looking for love and acceptance in the wrong places, outside of myself. I had completely neglected my relationship with myself in the process of ignoring the warning signs and overcompensating for others. It was time to start working seriously!

Sidenote on ignoring your relationship with Self

John Templeton, a philanthropist, once said, "It's nice to be important, but it's more important to be nice." Despite being a nice quote, this one is inaccurate and incomplete. First off, you cheat yourself out of authenticity when you act "nice" out of obligation rather than because it is in line with who you are as a person. Why should you have to act contrary to your beliefs and moral principles just to make someone happy? You don't, is the quick response. Second, dimming your light in order to avoid conflict or follow the crowd is the ultimate act of self-rejection because it amounts to saying that other people's opinions and desires are more important than your own, which, my friend, they are not. Here's my advice: the sooner you realise this and make the effort to love yourself more deeply, the better.

Getting back to the narrative…

There I was—a single woman in the depths of despair. My self-worth had formally moved out, and it wasn't pleasant. I did a great job of pretending my confidence was still there and that everything was fine, despite the unbearable weight of my mental and emotional anguish. It was time for me to put on my big-girl skirt and take a risk with this thing called self-love because I couldn't maintain the facade for much longer. Wow, I'm so happy I did.

I've learned self-love techniques, the value of gratitude, how to forgive myself and others, and how to use hypnosis, neuro-linguistic programming, and the mind-body connection to advance my professional growth over the past few years. Once you establish a connection with an unconditional love for yourself, it's amazing what you can bring into your life. The girl who ignored herself is long gone; she's now a mother of two children, is in a loving and emotionally mature relationship and has turned her passion for self-love and empowerment into a successful business.

What exactly is self-love, and how can you tell if you lack it?

As a result of the close relationship between self-love and self-worth (or value), it follows that when you don't value yourself as a person, you're more likely to judge yourself harshly, use critical self-talk, and neglect activities that nurture your mind, body, and soul. This may indicate that you frequently (but not always) live in a state of flight or fight and often feel depressed, anxious, or worthless.

Self-love is not based on a single deed or behaviour. It's not a place to get to ("Yes, I've arrived at self-love and can cross that off my bucket list!"), but rather a mindset that supports yourself by making decisions and taking actions that advance your physical, emotional, spiritual, and psychological well-being.

Using a straightforward example: You would undoubtedly feel absolutely amazing if you consistently exercised and followed a healthy diet in pursuit of your ideal body weight and shape. What would happen if you then decided that you were finished working out and eating well because you were so fit and gorgeous? In a year, would you still look and feel the same? Absolutely not. Your overall health would begin to reflect your new diet choice, and over time, your muscle tone would begin to soften.

The same can be said for loving oneself; it is a lifelong process that improves with time, becomes more fulfilling, and opens up more success and opportunities. It's a metaphorical muscle that loves to be flexed!

Here is a list of characteristics and behaviours that show whether you naturally show self-love or whether you unintentionally dim your light, if you are unsure of where you fall on the self-love spectrum.

Self-love	Dimming your light
Speaking your truth, even when others will judge you for it,	Silencing yourself to appease others.
Speaking kindly and constructively to yourself.	Criticising and putting yourself down.
Setting and upholding healthy boundaries.	Being a human doormat and not sticking up for yourself.
Spending time with people who make you happy and support you.	Hanging around people or situations that drain your energy and make you feel bad.
Resting when you're feeling unwell.	Pushing yourself to the point of burnout.
Showing up with courage.	Never taking a chance.
Being honest with yourself about your flaws and taking positive actions to improve them.	Punishing yourself for flaws or being a victim to them.
Appreciating and celebrating your wins.	Adopting the mindset that nothing you do is ever good enough.
Saying no to things that go against your values.	Saying yes to keep the peace and people-please.
Saying yes to things you want and that make you feel good.	Self-sabotaging things that would be great for you.

Acknowledging and embracing all your emotions.	Pushing negative feelings down so you don't have to deal with them.
Expressing gratitude.	Seeing the glass as half empty.
Taking advantage of opportunities.	Making excuses for why you can't do something.
Prioritising what's important to you.	Neglecting your wants and needs.
Being patient with yourself.	Getting frustrated with yourself.
Taking care of yourself.	Treating yourself poorly.
Learning something new.	Shutting yourself off to other points of view and possibilities.
Admitting when you're wrong and putting strategies in place to make things right.	Playing victim and living in denial.

Self-love is not selfish; rather, it is essential to the best possible state of your physical, mental, and emotional health. It involves getting to know yourself better, admitting that you're not a perfect person, and still being kind to and loving towards yourself. It involves recognising and appreciating all of your wonderful qualities, taking time to relax, and having the courage to push yourself. Saying no to things you don't want and yes to things that make you happy shows respect for yourself, even when others may not agree with you or may even judge you for it.

It took a lot of soul-searching and "getting real" with myself for me to replace everything that wasn't helping me grow—including my self-deprecating thoughts—with self-love routines that I can count on to help me learn and develop even on my worst days.

My transition from feeling helpless and insecure in life to displaying confidence, self-awareness, and resilience each day was made possible in large part by practising self-love techniques. I now instruct women all over the world on how to master their emotions and re-connect with themselves through the power of self-love practises, NLP, hypnotherapy, and TimeLine TherapyTM as an Emotional Mastery and Accountability Coach.

Who is at risk of lacking self-love?

All of us, to put it briefly.

Addiction, abuse, crippling social anxiety, toxic relationships, and self-harm are not always the fate of those who lack self-love. Yes, even though these instances scream for the need to boost one's sense of self-worth and love, reality also includes the other side of the coin. Many of the women who naturally exude confidence are those who I've assisted in developing their best sense of self-love and emotional resilience. These women were compassionate, driven, passionate, and successful; they merely had unconscious negative self-beliefs, insecurities, or trauma.

Sidenote on trauma

Trauma is frequently linked to traumatic, harsh experiences (like violent crime or serious illness), but it can also result from anything that makes people feel extremely distressed on a psychological or emotional level. It's important to keep in mind that trauma is subjective; what is traumatic for one person may not be for another. Trauma is divided into three groups, as follows:

Acute: brought on by a single occurrence (such as learning your partner cheated on you).

Chronic: resulting from prolonged and recurrent experiences (such as bullying).

Complex: exposure to numerous severe, invasive, and interpersonal events (such as child abuse or neglect).

Trauma negatively affects a person's thoughts and beliefs about themselves, making it challenging for them to love themselves because they frequently doubt their ability to overcome what happened, their ability to move on, or even that they are deserving of love in general.

HOW SELF-LOVE TOOK ANNA FROM VICTIM TO VICTORY

Anna had a wonderful life, with a loving family, a vivacious boyfriend, a job she loved, and a career path that was 90% near perfect. Except that she had been tied to a traumatic event in her past for years by a dark secret. The underlying shame and sadness continued to surface and influence her daily thoughts, emotional state, and even her relationships, even though she had dealt with her emotions as best she could and was moving on with her life. She reached out to me for assistance, which required courage and strength. She was finally able to break free from the emotional bonds of the trauma through a variety of therapy procedures and techniques and move into a state of self-acceptance, healing, and self-love. A few days after our final session, Anna texted to let me know she had recently gotten engaged and was ecstatic about the future she is now building. The energy you emit is obvious to everyone when you practise self-love and accept yourself without conditions. I recently got a message from Anna's mother thanking me for helping her daughter overcome hardship and flourish in an environment of love, joy, and positivity.

Every one of us is capable of loving ourselves. We all deserve to enjoy self-love.

FALL MADLY IN LOVE WITH YOURSELF IN THREE SIMPLE STEPS

What exactly are the self-love techniques and practices I've been talking so much about? I'd have to politely ask each author in this book to donate their pages in order to finish them all (and, to be honest, even that wouldn't be enough)!

No matter where you are on your self-love journey or whether you are new to the power of self-acceptance and appreciation, putting these three easy steps into practice in your life is a surefire way to increase your sense of self-worth, confidence, and happiness.

Are you prepared to...

Drop the old story that self-love is selfish and fill your self-love cup to the brim?

Make peace with your inner critic while recognising your incredible abilities?

Master self-love using the force of forgiveness?

Alicia Ann Wade

FILL YOUR SELF-LOVE CUP TO THE BRIM

As I mentioned earlier, in order to allow ourselves to truly shine and live a life we are madly in love with, self-love is a necessary component. Filling your cup refers to engaging in activities you enjoy that give you a positive sense of well-being, nourish your mind, body, and soul, and restore your energy so you can be the best version of yourself. There are countless things you can do to fill your cup, including going shopping for new shoes, scheduling a massage, sleeping in on Sunday mornings, going away with friends, taking a bath, and unwinding with your favourite book and cup of tea.

What happens if you don't fill your cup? Imagine this. You have a full cup of water, and your friend asks for a sip because he's thirsty. Sure, you think. And you give him a big gulp. You are about to take a sip yourself, but before you can, another thirsty friend comes over for a drink, and then another, and another. What happens if you don't fill your cup first?

If you're someone who enjoys helping others but needs persuasion to take care of yourself, what you're about to do may present a challenge, but I assure you that it will be worthwhile!

INSPO-ACTION

Take a moment to put the book down, get a pen and paper, and make a list of five things you can do this week to show yourself some L.O.V.E. Remember, the only requirement is that they involve something that brings you joy and nourishes your soul—they don't have to be expensive. You can include other people (for example, on a date night), but you must gain something solely for your happiness, development, or benefit.

Ready, set, go!

Now that you have your list, get out your calendar/diary and schedule them. If we don't make time for ourselves, no one else will. Decide now when you will do these things. I'll go first…

Saturday AM: Take a 20-minute break from housework to read a magazine.

Saturday PM: Buy an expensive brand of chocolate.

Sunday AM: 30 min sleep-in.

Monday PM (once the kids are asleep): Take a relaxing bath with essential oils.

Tuesday PM: Binge-watch my favourite Netflix show OR binge-watch my favourite Netflix show whilst eating expensive chocolate (bet you didn't think this exercise could get any better but voila, there you go!)

Wednesday AM: Take a stroll around the neighbourhood and enjoy nature.

Every AM: Look in the mirror and say something kind to myself.

Every PM: Use the expensive cutlery set usually reserved for guests (seriously, what have I been waiting for?!)

Ok, that's more than five, but I get excited when I see how simple it is to plan a little self-love time!

Think of filling your cup like using an oxygen mask on an aeroplane. You're advised, "If the masks drop, fit your own mask first before helping others." Why? Because there is no way you can help other people when you're struggling to breathe! And there's no way you can pour kindness, generosity, and love from an empty cup! Fill it daily and watch the love pour over for yourself and others.

SELF-LOVE MANTRA

Repeat this daily: "Flexing my self-love muscle increases my emotional fitness and nourishes my mind, body, and soul. It helps me embrace my needs, dial up my self-worth, and allows me to give from my overflow."

REMEMBER HOW AMAZING YOU ARE, INNER CRITIC

The opinions you hold about yourself are an insight into how likely you are to engage in self-love activities. Additionally, they establish the parameters for what you're prepared to put up with in life (also known as boundaries) and how you accept treatment from others.

Most of the time, negative thoughts about yourself are hidden in your subconscious mind, a region of your psyche. Your inner voice can be your best supporter ("Wow, you look great," "You can do it," etc.) or your worst critic ("I can't believe you said that," "You're such an idiot," etc.) when these opinions or thoughts come to you. We all constantly talk to ourselves, and for the most part, it is incredibly beneficial. But when our internal record player gets stuck on the same self-deprecating song, it can become damaging to our self-esteem and confidence. Our enthusiasm to practise self-love goes out the window.

To be clear, even though your subconscious mind does occasionally say horrible things, it's not trying to make you feel bad. Its primary goal is to keep you safe, and it accomplishes this by making comparisons between the present and the past in order to process and comprehend what is going on around you. Then it generates a series of ideas and feelings to lead you in the safest direction possible. Thus, underlying all your negative self-talk is a hidden desire to protect you from harm.

Nothing in life is perfect, and sometimes your subconscious mind interprets anything that is outside of your comfort zone as danger in an attempt to keep you safe. Because although new experiences are great for development, they can also be quite terrifying. Consider the possibility that you decide to switch careers. Although there is nothing obviously dangerous about that, your subconscious mind will quickly start weighing the advantages and disadvantages, resulting in a range of emotions from excitement and nervousness to fear and doubt. This leads to negative self-talk such as "Don't bother, you won't get it anyway" (danger, danger, the grass isn't greener on the other side) or "Go for it, you've got this" (it's safe to change jobs because you're awesome). Based on various evaluations of how "risky" the change is, both messages are motivated by a desire to keep you safe. And I'm sorry to break it to you, but this risk assessment process is directly influenced by how strong your self-love muscle is. Change is less frightening the more you value yourself because you will feel more confident that you can handle anything that comes your way.

The best way to boost your self-esteem right away is to recognise the wonderful traits that make you the distinctive person that you are!

INSPO-ACTION

Take a moment to put this book down, get a pen and paper, and begin making a list of the characteristics, qualities, and behaviours you admire about yourself. Before you cringe at the thought of doing this, stop judging yourself and just do it! You don't have to share this list with anyone.

There are no prerequisites for what you can include, and there are no correct answers to this. Include it on your list if you value your vision! Are you smart, a good cook, a dependable friend, a fun parent, tolerant, brave, and fantastic in bed? Write them all down, my friend!

Read your list each day and truly own your amazingness to get the most confidence-boosting benefits from this exercise. It will be much simpler for you to set boundaries with people and circumstances that are no longer beneficial to you once you realise how much you have to offer as a person.

Note

This list will always be growing because as you work on self-love, you'll discover more positive qualities about yourself that you can keep adding.

MASTER YOUR SELF-LOVE WITH THE POWER OF FORGIVENESS

Working through emotional baggage with the help of forgiveness—for yourself and others—is a big part of self-love.

We release negative emotions like guilt and shame and alter our internal dialogue when we forgive ourselves (for errors we've made or for doing wrong to others). By forgiving others for their mistakes, we lift the burdensome anchor that binds us to these incidents, and we let go of emotions like rage, sadness, and fear.

In no way does forgiving someone imply that you 'agree' with what has occurred or that it is acceptable for them to treat you badly. The other person doesn't matter at all. Giving yourself the green light to let go of things that are impeding your ability to advance mentally, emotionally, physically, and spiritually is what forgiveness is all about. Once you've let go, you'll experience emotional healing and freedom that makes it possible to understand, accept, and love yourself on a deeper level.

In all the years I have coached people on this topic, Ho'oponopono, a traditional Hawaiian practice of reconciliation and forgiveness, has proven to be the most potent and effective technique I have ever encountered. The meditation's fundamental goal is to restore equilibrium, and in practice, it serves as both a tool for peacemaking and a mantra for self-love.

Ho'oponopono does not require any training. It is a gentle meditation comprised of four simple steps:

Repentance - repeat "I'm sorry."

Forgiveness - repeat "Please forgive me."

Gratitude - repeat "Thank you."

Love - repeat "I love you."

INSPO-ACTION

Close your eyes, take a few deep breaths, and concentrate on what you want to let go of or who you want to forgive (keep in mind that you might be the person you want to forgive). You should feel all the feelings that are connected to that event come to the surface inside of you; allow them to do so, stay present in them, and cry if necessary. This is a natural part of the healing process.

Then, slowly repeat to yourself…

I'M SORRY
PLEASE FORGIVE ME
THANK YOU
I LOVE YOU

Repeat ten times.

Depending on the circumstance, you might feel a release of emotions right away or you might need to incorporate Ho'oponopono into your daily routine over the course of several months. No matter how long it takes, practising Ho'oponopono every day will enable you to let go of the past through the power of emotional freedom and forgiveness, creating a clear path for you to foster greater self-love and acceptance.

CHAPTER SUMMARY

The most important relationship you will ever have is the one you have with yourself.

Do not place your worth in the hands of other people.

The ability to set boundaries is facilitated by self-love practices that increase self-esteem and confidence.

Fill your self-love cup every day, even if it's just by doing the smallest thing. Real change and transformation come from consistently doing these things.

You can easily increase your level of self-love by engaging in activities like:

Scheduling 'Me Time' in your calendar. Enjoyable activities that allow you to relax, have fun and grow don't have to cost anything but are invaluable to your emotional health and mental well-being.

Writing a list of qualities you love about yourself, and getting into the habit of acknowledging and appreciating what makes you an amazing person boosts your confidence and self-esteem. It also encourages your inner dialogue to be positive and supportive.

Ho'oponopono: a traditional Hawaiian meditation for forgiveness, self-love, and emotional freedom.

Alicia Ann Wade

To dial up your self-love and master your emotions with more techniques, contact me here:

Instagram - www.instagram.com/lisainfante.coach
Facebook - www.facebook.com/thegoddesscodecoaching
Website - www.thegoddesscode.com.au

CHAPTER 16

Embrace Self Love

Christine Innes

"Embracing self-love and knowing and understanding it are two different things."

When we talk about self-love, what do we know and understand about it?

The word "self" according to the Cambridge dictionary is "the set of someone's characteristics, such as personality and ability, that are not physical and make that person different from other people"

The word "love" according to the Cambridge dictionary is "to like another adult very much and be romantically and sexually attracted to them, or to have strong feelings of liking a friend or person in your family"

When combining the two words they make quite a powerful combination.

As human beings, we are social creatures who thrive on connection with others. We are wired to seek validation, recognition, and love from those around us. We are often taught from a young age to prioritize the needs and wants of others before our own. We learn to give generously to our families, friends, and communities, often without a second thought. However, we are not always taught the importance of giving back to ourselves, by prioritising self-love, and self-care.

Self-love is a concept that can be difficult to understand and even harder to put into practice. It involves recognizing our worth, acknowledging our strengths and weaknesses, and treating ourselves with compassion, kindness, and respect. It requires us to prioritize our own needs, wants, and desires, even when it feels uncomfortable or goes against what we have been taught.

The idea of putting ourselves first can be uncomfortable because it goes against what we have been taught. We may feel guilty or selfish for taking time to focus on ourselves when there are so many others in our lives who need our attention. We may fear that if we prioritize ourselves, we will be seen as self-centred or uncaring.

However, prioritizing self-love is not selfish. It is essential to our well-being and happiness. When we take care of ourselves, we are better able to care for those around us. When we prioritize self-love, we are better equipped to set boundaries, communicate our needs, and make decisions that align with our values.

Learning to love ourselves can be a lifelong journey. It requires us to unlearn old habits and beliefs, and to rewire our brains to prioritize self-care. We may need to seek out support, whether it's from friends, family, or a therapist, to help us on this journey.

The concept of self-love is not a new one, yet it is something that many of us struggle with. Growing up in the '80s and 90's, the focus was on the ideal body type, the "perfect" appearance, and fitting into a certain mould. This pressure to conform to a certain standard left many young girls feeling inadequate, unworthy, and unable to fully embrace themselves. As someone who grew up in this era, I can relate to these feelings all too well.

For me, the pressure to fit in started at a young age. I was an overweight girl, and I quickly learned that I didn't fit into the mould that society had created for young women. The focus was on being thin, having a thigh gap, and looking like the models on the covers of Cosmopolitan and Vogue magazines. I tried to change myself to fit in, going on diets and trying to lose weight, but nothing seemed to work.

As I got older, the pressure to fit in only intensified. I was constantly bombarded with images of "perfect" women on social media and in magazines. I felt like I wasn't good enough, and that I needed to change who I was in order to fit in. It wasn't until I turned 40 that I began to realise that this way of thinking was not serving me positively or healthily.

So, I began to question why I was putting so much energy into changing myself to fit into a mould that was not designed for me. Why was I trying to be someone else when I could simply be myself?

This realization was a turning point for me, and I decided to fully embrace who I was.

At the age of 45, after years of dieting and trying to change my appearance, I finally decided to stop. I realized that the only way to truly love myself was to accept myself exactly as I was. This was a radical concept for me, as I had spent my entire life trying to change who I was.

I made a conscious decision to step fully into myself, to embrace my skin, my thoughts, and my ideas. I decided to play full out, to stop worrying about what others thought of me, and to start living my life on my terms.

This decision was not an easy one, and it required a lot of work on my part. I had to unlearn years of negative self-talk, and I had to learn to love myself for who I was, not for who I thought I should be. I had to let go of the idea that I needed to change myself in order to fit in, and I had to learn to embrace my unique qualities and quirks – I had to learn how to fall in love with myself – flaws and all.

Through this journey of self-love, I have learned that true love starts with accepting yourself exactly as you are. It means not judging yourself for your looks, your thoughts, your ideas, the way you speak, or the way you dress. It means embracing all parts of yourself, even the parts that you may consider "flaws." It means realizing that you are worthy of love and acceptance, simply because you exist.

Learning to love yourself is not a one-time event, but rather a lifelong journey. It requires consistent effort and a willingness to let go of old patterns and beliefs. It means learning to prioritize your own needs and desires, even when it feels uncomfortable or goes against what you have been taught.

If you are struggling with self-love, know that you are not alone. It is a common struggle and one that requires patience, compassion, and a willingness to learn. Start by taking small steps every day to prioritize your own needs, whether it's taking time for yourself, practising self-compassion, setting boundaries, or engaging in activities that bring you joy.

Yet what changed?

Firstly, it is that I have now surrounded myself with my own tribe. A tribe of incredible, powerful, accepting women and men who see me for me. No more pretending, trying to be someone else, as I am enough who I am. This has been key for me, especially as a female entrepreneur.

Secondly, when my dad passed away last year, it was like a wake-up call of how precious life is. Time is short and the only infinite thing is death. So, I took this new lease on life and ran with it. I stepped into gratitude for every single day I am here and embraced life with a new and exciting outlook and learning to love and trust myself more each day, as at the of our life, the only thing we can take with us is our memories and our self-respect and love.

Thirdly, as a female entrepreneur, one must embrace self-love. It helps in creating a positive mindset, boosting confidence, and promoting self-care.

Embracing self-love and knowing and understanding it are two different things.

So how can we embrace self-love?

Practice self-awareness. This is the foundation of self-love. It involves paying attention to your thoughts, emotions, and behaviour – the good and not so good and doing it without judgement. This awareness helps in identifying patterns that might be holding you back and developing new positive patterns that align with your goals in life and values.

I find I can practice self-awareness by journaling, mediation or even speaking to a coach or therapist.

Self-compassion. This involves treating ourselves with kindness and understanding. Most of us treat our best friends better than we do ourselves. Going deeper than treating yourself with love, kindness and understanding it is also acknowledging and accepting our mistakes and learning from them as a part of forgiveness. Forgiving ourselves is a way we can allow more goodness into our lives and let go of our shame and guilt.

Setting boundaries. This is essential. Boundaries protect our time, energy, love, and well-being. As an entrepreneur, our business journey can pull us in so many different directions, and knowing our boundaries show us respect for ourselves and we are also showing others how we should be treated.

Gratitude and keep it flowing. The more you are grateful for yourself, your life and even the challenges you have faced, it opens you up to heal wounds and give back the love to yourself.

As more and more women are becoming entrepreneurs, it is important to understand the challenges they face. One of the biggest struggles that female entrepreneurs face is self-love

Societal conditioning plays a major role in the lack of self-love among female entrepreneurs. Women are often conditioned to put others before themselves and to prioritize their families and relationships over their own needs. This societal expectation can lead to feelings of guilt and inadequacy when women pursue their entrepreneurial goals, especially if it means taking time away from their families. Women may feel that they are not fulfilling their role in society as a caregiver and may even feel guilty for pursuing their passions.

A lack of representation of women in leadership roles can also impact the self-love of female entrepreneurs. In the business world, men have traditionally held leadership roles and have been seen as the standard of success. This can make it difficult for women to feel confident in their abilities and may lead to imposter syndrome, where women feel like they are not good enough or qualified enough to be successful. This lack of strong female role models can make it difficult for women to see themselves as successful entrepreneurs, which can impact their self-love.

The pressure to conform to traditional beauty standards, especially in advertising, social media and society, can also impact the self-love of female entrepreneurs. Women are often judged based on their appearance and may feel like they need to conform to certain beauty standards in order to be successful. This can lead to feelings of inadequacy and self-doubt, especially if women do not fit into the traditional mould of what a successful entrepreneur looks like.

Fear of failure can also impact self-love for female entrepreneurs. Women may feel like they have more to lose if their business fails, especially if they have invested a lot of time and money into their business and put this first before family and friends.

The impact of self-love and the lack of self-love is signification for female entrepreneurs. It can affect their ability to take risks and pursue their dreams, goals and can limit their success. The feelings of self-doubt, and inadequacy can also impact their mental health and well-being.

There are several ways a female entrepreneur can improve their own relationship with self-love.

Take time out and prioritise yourself.

Advocating for themselves and not allowing the judgement from self and others to come into play.

Redefine success and what that looks like for yourself.

The lack of self-love among female entrepreneurs is a significant challenge that must be addressed. By understanding the societal conditioning, lack of representation, pressure to conform to beauty standards, and fear of failure that impact self-love, female entrepreneurs can take steps to prioritize self-care, challenge societal biases, and redefine success on their own terms. By doing so, female entrepreneurs can improve their mental health and well-being, and ultimately achieve greater success in their entrepreneurial ventures.

To ensure that we are giving back to ourselves, practising self-love comes back to understanding the two key words: Self and Love.

Remind ourselves each day of the key role we play in our own lives – we are the main character and it is time we put ourselves up on the pedestal and give everything a bit of goodness to ourselves as we can.

Show love, love and more love to ourselves each day. We cannot expect others to know how to love us if we don't know how to give it to ourselves.

Knowing this and embracing it is the way forward.

Step into the best version of yourself and treat yourself like the queen or king that you are and embrace yourself because you are one of a kind.

CHAPTER 17

Self-Compassion is Self-Love

Shanki Jayawickrama

"Embarking on a self-love journey is a transformative path towards personal growth and fulfillment."

I picked up 2 suitcases and picked up my 1year and 3 months old baby, had one last look at the house I made at home , left the key under the mat, took a taxi and left , never to come back. This turned out to be my Greatest Journey towards self love while honouring the life I left behind because I had to leave a space that was not a space of values match for Me. I needed to remove myself in order to create a better life for me and my son.

In a bold, transformative decision, I made my divorce a testament to love and celebration. Instead of dwelling on bitterness or resentment, I shifted my perspective and embraced the opportunity for growth and renewal. It was on the 14th of February, a day traditionally associated with love, Valentine's Day to be exact, that I applied for the divorce. This symbolic act represented my commitment to approaching this transition with grace and compassion. By choosing love over animosity, I opened the door for healing and new beginnings. I recognized that even in the face of endings, there is room for love and celebration, for honoring the lessons learned and embracing the possibilities that lie ahead.

When it came to child support, I made a personal decision not to apply or ask for it from my ex-husband. It was a choice rooted in my own circumstances and beliefs. While I hold deep respect for those who choose to pursue child support, I recognized that I did not require it for myself. My ex generously offered support, but I felt a sense of independence and self-sufficiency that allowed me to provide for my child without relying on him for financial assistance. This decision was not about diminishing the importance of child support, but rather a reflection of my unique situation and my ability to meet the needs of my child on my own. It was a choice made with thoughtful consideration and an understanding that different paths work for different families.

In the days that followed, I immersed myself in self-reflection and self-improvement. I enrolled in classes to enhance my professional skills, determined to excel in my career, and create a life of financial independence. I surrounded myself with positive influences and sought guidance from mentors who believed in my potential.

The turning point in my journey came when I embraced self-acceptance wholeheartedly. I made a conscious decision to accept myself as a single mother, recognizing that my circumstances did not define my worth. This acceptance empowered me to establish healthy boundaries, ensuring that I surrounded myself only with people who uplifted and supported me. I cleared my contacts, intentionally distancing myself from individuals who were unresourceful or brought negativity into my life. Instead, I chose to be in the company of those who would cheer me on, seeking support and guidance from coaches who could help me navigate my path. I also focused on developing emotional intimacy, understanding that true connection starts from within.

I worked tirelessly to create the life I desired, and to build the business I envisioned. Along the way, I learned to cultivate more compassion for myself, embracing failure as a natural part of growth and allowing myself to be vulnerable. I came to realize that I was not alone in my experiences as a single mother or as someone who had gone through a divorce. I embraced my authentic self, understanding that my uniqueness mattered. I took ownership of my future, knowing that it was in my hands to shape and create, and that I had the power to cultivate self-love, self-acceptance, and gratitude within myself. I realized that certainty and validation were not dependent on external factors but could be nurtured and developed internally. I expanded my understanding to include that all of this growth and transformation could occur within me.

Of course, there were setbacks along the way. I faced numerous failures and encountered moments of self-doubt. But I had learned that failure was not an indication of defeat, but rather a stepping stone toward success. With each setback, I analyzed the situation, learned from my mistakes, and adjusted my approach.

As time passed, I discovered hidden talents and passions that had long been suppressed. I pursued my interests with coaching, couselling, holistic counselling, emotional intelligence, emotional intimacy, and human behaviour. These activities became outlets for my emotions and sources of inspiration, allowing me to channel my experiences into something beautiful.

The journey of self-discovery and independence was not without its challenges, but the more I invested in myself, the more I realized my worth. I surrounded myself with a support network of friends and family who cheered me on, every step of the way. Their unwavering belief in me fueled my determination to create the life I had always dreamed of.

It was then that my own mother, a wise and experienced woman, imparted an invaluable lesson. She reminded me of the importance of putting my needs first, not as a selfish act, but as a necessary step towards self-care and personal growth. She shared stories of her own journey as a mother and how she had learned that looking after yourself creates wonderful relationships around you and also creates her own well-being ultimately affecting her ability to be the best parent she could be.

Her words resonated deeply within me, stirring a longing to reclaim my own identity and prioritize my own needs. I understood that by taking care of myself, I would be able to show up as a happier, more fulfilled mother for my children. It was a shift in perspective that allowed me to embrace self-care without guilt or hesitation.

With my mother's guidance, I began to carve out moments of solitude and self-reflection. I engaged in activities that brought me joy and rejuvenation, whether it was reading a book, going for walks, or indulging in a hobby like self-development, one I had long neglected. I learned that these moments of self-nourishment were not indulgent luxuries, but rather essential investments in my own well-being.

Through this journey of self-discovery, I also imparted valuable lessons to my child. I showed him that it was important to honor and respect oneself, to set boundaries, and to pursue their passions and dreams. By witnessing their mother prioritize her own well-being, they learned the importance of self-love and self-care, preparing them for their own journeys of personal growth and fulfillment.

Looking back, I am grateful for the wisdom my mother shared with me. She taught me that being a mother doesn't mean sacrificing my own happiness and dreams. Instead, it means finding a harmonious balance between nurturing my child and nurturing myself. And in doing so, I discovered that by putting my needs first, I could create a life filled with love, joy, and fulfillment for both myself and my child.

Suppressing my emotions led me down a path of unhealthy coping mechanisms, particularly binge eating. When I allowed myself to indulge in this behavior, I found temporary solace. In good moods, I convinced myself that everything was fine. But during the lows, it became evident that binge eating was not a great solution. To counterbalance the effects of overeating, I abused the gym, fixating on staying physically fit. However, as I delved deeper into my journey, I realized the need to address the underlying issues causing this pattern. I began studying weight management, holistic counseling & coaching and invested in my own personal development. I allowed myself to learn and create, embracing growth along the way. Through education and self-investment, I gradually let go of the woman I once was and emerged as the woman I am today.

Recognizing the importance of self-compassion was not an overnight realization but rather a gradual understanding that unfolded through introspection and self-reflection. I had always been quick to criticize myself, holding impossibly high standards and berating myself for any perceived shortcomings. However, as I embarked on this journey of personal growth, I came to understand that self-compassion was not a weakness but a strength—a way to cultivate resilience and foster inner kindness.

Self-compassion involves treating oneself with the same warmth, understanding, and care that one would offer a dear friend or loved one. It encompasses embracing one's flaws, accepting one's humanity, and acknowledging that making mistakes and facing challenges is an inherent part of the human experience.

Through self-compassion, I learned to embrace my imperfections and view failures as opportunities for growth. Instead of being my own harshest critic, I became a nurturing and supportive voice in my own life. I learned to extend kindness and understanding to myself, especially during moments of difficulty or setbacks. This shift in mindset allowed me to approach challenges with greater resilience, self-acceptance, and emotional well-being.

Research on self-compassion has shown its numerous benefits on mental health, emotional well-being, and interpersonal relationships. Studies have demonstrated that individuals who practice self-compassion experience reduced levels of anxiety, depression, and self-criticism. They also tend to have higher levels of self-esteem, optimism, and life satisfaction.

Self-compassion has also been linked to healthier coping mechanisms and improved emotional regulation. By being kind to oneself in times of distress, individuals are more likely to respond to difficult emotions with patience and understanding, rather than falling into patterns of self-destructive behavior or negative self-talk.

Furthermore, self-compassion plays a vital role in nurturing healthy relationships. When we cultivate self-compassion, we develop a greater capacity for empathy, understanding, and compassion towards others. It becomes easier to relate to the struggles and challenges faced by our loved ones, fostering deeper connections and fostering a supportive, non-judgmental environment.

In my own journey, self-compassion has allowed me to approach myself and others with greater empathy and understanding. It has helped me navigate the ups and downs of life with a sense of grace and self-acceptance. By extending compassion to myself, I have also learned to offer the same kindness and empathy to those around me, cultivating stronger and more fulfilling relationships.

Self-compassion is not a one-time practice but an ongoing commitment to oneself. It involves creating a space of love, acceptance, and understanding within our own hearts. It matters because it enables us to foster resilience, promote emotional well-being, and cultivate healthier connections with ourselves and others.

As I continue on my journey of self-discovery, self-compassion remains an integral part of my growth. It is a constant reminder to treat myself with gentleness, embrace my humanness, and extend the same understanding and kindness to others. Through self-compassion, I have found a source of strength, healing, and transformation—an essential ingredient in creating a life filled with love, authenticity, and personal fulfillment.

Gratitude became an essential component of my journey as I recognized the need to let go of what no longer served me and build the life I truly desired. I expressed gratitude for having the courage to acknowledge the aspects of my life that were not aligning with my values and for having the strength to release them. It was a profound act of self-love and empowerment.

With a newfound sense of clarity, I made the conscious decision to remove myself from groups and associations that no longer supported my growth and well-being.

By intentionally seeking out communities, friendships, and networks that resonated with my values and aspirations, I opened myself up to new possibilities. These groups provided me with the support, encouragement, and knowledge I needed to thrive. The individuals within these circles celebrated my growth and shared their own wisdom, pushing me to continually evolve and reach new heights.

This shift in my social landscape allowed me to expand my horizons, broaden my perspectives, and gain valuable insights from like-minded individuals. It was liberating to connect with people who shared my passions, dreams, and aspirations, as we inspired and motivated one another to pursue our goals fearlessly. The collective energy of these groups propelled me forward on my journey of self-discovery, instilling a renewed sense of purpose and empowerment.

Gratitude served as a guiding light, reminding me to appreciate the courage it took to detach myself from what no longer served me and embrace a new path of growth and authenticity. It was a reminder to honor my own worth and create boundaries that protected my well-being. As I practiced gratitude for these transformative changes, I cultivated a deep sense of self-respect and resilience.

With every step I took, I acknowledged and expressed gratitude for the courage to let go, for the opportunities that lay ahead, and for the unwavering belief in myself. Gratitude became a powerful tool that fueled my determination to build the life I desired—a life rooted in alignment with my values, passions, and purpose.

In this new chapter of my journey, gratitude continued to guide me, reminding me to appreciate each experience, whether challenging or joyful. It allowed me to see the beauty in the lessons learned and the growth that unfolded. Gratitude became a source of strength, reminding me that I had the power to create the life I envisioned, surrounded by individuals who uplifted and inspired me.

As I reflect on this transformative process, I am grateful for the opportunity to shed what no longer served me, cultivate gratitude for my own growth, and intentionally connect with communities that nourish my soul. It is through this journey of self-discovery, guided by gratitude, that I continue to build a life that aligns with my truest self and brings me profound joy, fulfillment, and a sense of purpose.

There are 6 pillars:

1. **Self-Acceptance**
2. **Self love**
3. **Gratitude**
4. **Hope**
5. **Believe**
6. **Courage**

Embarking on a self-love journey is a transformative path towards personal growth and fulfillment. It begins with embracing the fundamental pillar of self-love, where we learn to cherish and honor ourselves unconditionally. With self-love as our guiding light, we open our hearts to gratitude, recognizing the abundance that surrounds us and shifting our focus towards the positive aspects of life. In moments of uncertainty, hope becomes our steadfast companion, illuminating the path ahead and reminding us of the endless possibilities that lie within our reach. Belief in ourselves and our dreams propels us forward, fueling our motivation and pushing us to overcome obstacles.

It takes immense courage to step outside our comfort zones, but with bravery as our armor, we can conquer our fears and embrace growth and change. Along this journey, self-compassion acts as our gentle guide, teaching us to be kind to ourselves during moments of struggle and offering solace and forgiveness when we stumble. With each step, we cultivate personal growth, unlocking our true potential and living a life filled with love, gratitude, hope, belief, courage, and self-compassion.

Alicia Ann Wade

My journey of testing my limits and pushing myself to new heights was a profound exploration of self-discovery and self-awareness. I embarked on this path to challenge myself, to see if I had truly grown and evolved from the person I used to be. As I ventured into uncharted territories, I confronted my inner demons and faced them head-on. They were no longer obstacles to be feared; instead, they became nourishment for my growth. In testing my limits, I attracted situations and opportunities that mirrored my past self, serving as reminders of who I once was. But in those moments, I recognized the transformation that had taken place within me. I realized that I had become resilient, courageous, and more determined than ever before. Each test was an invitation to evaluate my progress, to see if I was aligning with the person I aspired to be. And through this process, I discovered that I was capable of surpassing my own expectations, embracing my true potential, and carving a path towards a brighter future.

I came to understand that self-love is not about punishing oneself to conform to societal ideals or pretending to be someone I'm not. It is not about putting on a facade and speaking empty words. I had engaged in these behaviors, believing that looking good was a form of punishment for myself and that vulnerability meant standing up for myself without having any boundaries. But self-love does not mean conforming to society's standards. I had mistakenly believed that fitting in would diminish my sense of inadequacy, that I needed to find external validation to shine. The truth is, I finally said, "Screw it all!" and accepted myself for the woman I truly am.

As I became stronger as an individual, I also held a safe and supportive space for others. The bonds I had lost along the way were rekindled, but with a newfound sense of peace. I formed stronger connections, based on love, compassion, and mutual respect for our individual journeys and values. We learned to honor each other's boundaries, bringing a sense of harmony and peace to our relationships.

In my wildest dreams, I never imagined that certain relationships would have the power to impact everyone involved in such profound ways. Through the ups and downs of my journey, I became an even better coach, equipped with a deeper understanding of how to serve my clients with certainty and vulnerability. By sharing my own experiences and being open about my own vulnerabilities, I created a safe space for others to do the same and create the lives they truly desired.

This journey has been incredibly fulfilling and continues to evolve, as I cultivate self-acceptance and compassion within myself. Having only lived in Australia for seven years, I am astounded by the greatness of my life, even without the physical presence of my family. I am teaching my son and many other women the power of standing strong on their own, demonstrating that a fulfilling and abundant life is possible regardless of external circumstances. Through sharing my truth, I am able to bring light and inspiration to other women and men alike. It all started with one powerful "yes" to myself, setting in motion a chain of transformative events that continue to shape and uplift countless lives.

CHAPTER 18

Self-love is a Lifelong Journey That Demands Patience, Commitment, and Ongoing Self-Care

Ali Moustafa

"Embrace self-love ultimately rests with each individual"

In our vast world, numerous opinions and guides abound, offering assistance and guidance to individuals on how to embark on the journey of self-love and how to take the necessary steps towards it. These resources aim to create a personalized path for each person, catering to their unique needs. However, ultimately, it is up to each individual to make the decision whether they are ready to embrace self-love.

You are distinct, exceptional, and unparalleled. Although you may share physical similarities with others, your spiritual essence cannot be replicated. Your soul, intangible yet palpable, emanates an energy that can be felt from afar. This realization serves as the foundation for understanding yourself. Without truly knowing who you are, it becomes impossible to truly love yourself. To be authentic, you must wholeheartedly believe in your own worth. Embracing self-love requires accepting every aspect of yourself, flaws, and all. This marks the beginning of a genuine and profound love for oneself.

Love is a concept that we often discuss, assuming we fully comprehend its meaning. Yet, love takes on different forms for each person. It manifests uniquely in appearance and sensation, shaped by our individual perspectives. As we embark on the journey of seeking love, we must pause and ask ourselves: Is this desire truly what we want, or is it a reflection of our genuine needs? If it is a want, we should contemplate its significance and the value it holds in the present moment. On the other hand, if it is a need, we should ponder the value it will bring to this beautiful world both now and in every fleeting moment we are blessed with life.

Love is undeniably a beautiful gift, perhaps one of the most important ones we can give ourselves and others. However, we must comprehend its meaning within ourselves first and foremost before we freely express it to those we care about. To understand love, we must embark on a journey of self-discovery. We need to cultivate a deep respect for who we are as individuals and learn to forgive ourselves for the past events that we continue to hold onto, despite having served their purpose in our lives. I am intimately familiar with this struggle, as I have lived through it myself. I experienced a profound sense of being lost and bewildered, uncertain about my emotions and identity. I believed that conforming to societal standards would bring me a sense of completeness, acceptance, and belonging. I chased after validation, acceptance, and love, all the things one desires until I reached a breaking point.

It was during this moment of crisis that I crashed into a metaphorical wall, falling onto an even harder floor. This jolt awakened me from my daze and broke the spell of societal hypnosis. I began to question my very existence and rediscover the essence of who I truly was. I examined the beliefs and values that shaped me, seeking to understand their origins and whether they still aligned with my authentic self. Through this introspective process, I unravelled the true meaning of love for myself.

I realized that my relentless pursuit of external love was, in fact, a manifestation of my deep longing for self-love. I understood that true love begins from within, nurturing a genuine appreciation and acceptance of oneself. This transformative realization allowed me to embark on a journey of self-love, where I discovered the immense power and fulfilment that comes from loving oneself authentically.

Initially, I held the belief that if I loved everyone unconditionally, I would find a sense of completeness, love, and inner peace. However, I soon realized that this notion was far from the truth. Confronting the rawness and honesty within myself was a challenging endeavour, but it was an essential step on my path. It revealed to me a profound realization: How could I genuinely love anyone else if I didn't first know how to love myself? Without understanding the true essence of self-love, my understanding of love itself was incomplete. It made me question the value of my existence. How could I be of any worth if I couldn't wholeheartedly give myself the love and care I deserved?

In this quest for self-discovery, I began to explore my fears and their origins. Were they inherent within me, or were they the result of generational trauma passed down through my family line? What were these fears, and why did they hold such power over me? It was a perplexing realization because I had a good childhood. I was fortunate to have loving parents who were migrants and understood the value of hard work. They came from a humble village, striving for a better life, and they bestowed upon us everything they could. As the 11th child out of 16, I couldn't be more grateful, thankful, and blessed for the love and support they provided.

Material possessions were never our focus, as we didn't have the latest fashionable clothes or gadgets. But that was inconsequential because what truly mattered was the safe space and nurturing environment they created for us. As the years went by, our relationships evolved and blossomed, unfolding in beautiful ways. However, there was one aspect that always intrigued me—how could my parents talk to each other every night? It amazed me, sometimes even rattled me, as I pondered the depth of their connection and communication.

I, as a child, would often yearn to sneak out, puzzled by how my parents could engage in lengthy conversations every single night. It seemed incomprehensible to me at the time. However, as I grew more attuned to myself and the world around me, I came to understand the significance of those conversations. To my parents, those nights of intimate dialogue were an expression of love. It was through witnessing this consistent act that I realized its profound impact on me. It surpassed the value of material gifts, weekend getaways, or shared experiences like visiting the trash n' treasure market with my dad, or observing my mother and sisters prepare a meal while we all came together.

It was the simple act of my parents conversing every night that left the most indelible mark on my heart and mind. It laid the foundation for my understanding of love. Moreover, it helped me unravel the fears that I had crafted within my own mind. These fears stemmed from doubting my own worthiness of love, not from others, but from myself. I questioned whether I was good enough, whether I possessed enough strength. However, as I delved deeper into my introspection, I began to perceive a glimmer of light amidst the darkness. It was that radiant light you can only see when surrounded by obscurity. It was the exquisite beauty that can only be found in the depths of darkness. And within that illumination, I discovered the true meaning of love for myself.

Through this profound journey, I realized that I am special, not in comparison to anyone else, but for the unique individual I am. It was through embracing self-love that I truly comprehended my own worth and recognized the extraordinary nature that resides within me.

It is an incredible realization that every single person is inherently perfect, not for the sake of others, but for themselves. Once we release the need to constantly please others and shift our focus inward, the energy we radiate begins to exude love, kindness, compassion, and care. When we truly love ourselves, our love becomes a radiant beacon, shining brightly for all to see. It is as if we carry an aura around us, emitting the very qualities we desire to see in the world.

Through the journey of self-love, we experience newfound freedom. We break free from the shackles that have bound us, and our perspective expands. Our eyes open wider, allowing us to see the beauty that surrounds us, and our breath becomes fuller, symbolizing a deep sense of liberation. Love takes on a unique meaning for each person, and it becomes the shield that protects us, the force that sets us free, and the purpose that ignites our souls.

As a single father, I have witnessed and experienced an abundance of life's joys and challenges. I poured my heart and soul into my responsibilities, giving my all to provide and care for my loved ones. However, in the process of dedicating myself to others, I unintentionally neglected my own needs. I worked tirelessly for something external, yet I failed to work hard enough to nurture and prioritize my well-being.

But now, through the wisdom gained from my experiences, I have come to realize the paramount importance of self-love. I understand that by nourishing and cherishing myself, I can better serve those around me. By valuing my worth and taking care of my own needs, I am able to show up as a more present, compassionate, and authentic version of myself for my loved ones. This newfound understanding has transformed my journey as a single father, reminding me of the significance of self-love in creating a fulfilling and harmonious life.

I grappled with the challenge of letting go of what I believed I wanted, only to realize that I had forgotten what I truly needed. I embarked on a search, seeking a quick fix to fill the void within me. Yet, I failed to recognize that the answers I sought were within myself all along. Now, I understand the importance of loving myself first and foremost. By doing so, I set an example of self-worth and self-belief, demonstrating to my son that loving who we are is essential, regardless of the circumstances we face.

The love we give our children knows no bounds. It is boundless and infinite. There is never a point where our love becomes too much or insufficient. Similarly, there are no limits to the love we should extend to ourselves, especially during difficult times. We should offer ourselves unwavering support, compassion, and understanding. There are no restrictions on the love we can share when someone needs a shoulder to cry on or a listening ear. And there are no limits to the love we hold deep within our souls, enabling us to forgive ourselves for our past mistakes and shortcomings.

One day, my son will embark on his unique path and discover what love means to him. He will build relationships with people who hold immense significance in his life. Throughout his journey, I will never cease to show him what love means to me. Just as my parents demonstrated their understanding of love, I will serve as a guiding light, imparting wisdom and teaching him the importance of self-love and the unconditional love we can offer others.

By embracing self-love and sharing its significance with my son, I hope to inspire him to cultivate a deep appreciation and acceptance of himself. I want him to understand that love begins from within and radiates outward, shaping the way we engage with the world and the relationships we form. Through my actions and words, I aim to instil in him the transformative power of love and its ability to create a more compassionate, empathetic, and harmonious existence.

In the vast landscape of self-love, numerous resources and guidance exist, offering assistance to individuals seeking to embark on this transformative journey. However, the decision to embrace self-love ultimately rests with each individual. It requires an understanding of one's unique essence and a genuine acceptance of oneself.

To cultivate self-love, it is essential to reflect on personal needs, prioritize self-care, and nurture physical, emotional, and mental well-being. Looking within and embracing one's uniqueness are crucial steps towards self-love. Setting healthy boundaries, practising self-compassion, and engaging in self-reflection are vital for developing a loving relationship with oneself. Additionally, forgiveness, self-discovery, and sharing love with others contribute to the cultivation of self-love.

Remember that self-love is a lifelong journey that demands patience, commitment, and ongoing self-care. Embrace the process and be kind to yourself along the way. By cultivating self-love, you not only create a more fulfilling and harmonious life for yourself but also serve as an inspiration to others, especially those you hold dear, fostering a world where love, compassion, and acceptance abound.

CHAPTER 19

The Pseudo Russian Princess

Alexandra De La Cruz

"I've come to learn that one's intuition is the greatest teacher, and trusting it is a gift of self-love, allowing me to just flow."

A long time ago in a land far, far away there was a Russian princess named Alexandra! Oops wait, that's a fairytale, wait, is it? Or is that my fairytale? Why don't we read on and see?

I started my life in Sandringham, Victoria. A beautiful beachside suburb in Melbourne. The day of my arrival was quite unexpected. I weighed 2 pounds 2 ounces and was born 10 weeks early. My dad has said I could fit in the palm of his hand, and he is a tall man (6'4") so he has quite large hands! I spent the next few months at the hospital in a humidicrib which they were called back in the day, growing strong and healthy everyday so I could rejoin my parents at home.

I don't remember much of my childhood, that's not to say that it was traumatic or that I had trauma. I just don't and to me that's okay. I

Self-Love

do have little snippets of memories, family holidays to Gunnamatta or other coastal holiday places where families would gather to enjoy the typical school holidays, sun, sand and surf. Camping in tents or travelling in caravans. Kids spent hours playing together in the outdoors, laughing and enjoying life before the complexities of life took over and we could no longer take the time. One trip we put the car on the train in Melbourne at Spencer Street Station and travelled across our beautiful land all the way to Adelaide where we disembarked, including the car! We then proceeded to drive across the Nullabor. Stopping wherever the mood took my parents to those quaint little places making happy family memories. Now I look back, I really believe that's where the love for my country took its roots, still to this day I would rather trek through my own land than to venture outside of it.

There was always the "absence" emotionally and mentally of my mum which was often due to her declining mental health, physical health or escalation of her addiction due to her health. There was a revolving door of rehab and hospitalization and our family lived in the shadow of mum's crises and happiness. In hindsight, I now know the struggles one faces to cope with declining mental health without alcohol and drugs and without adequate support.

I had a pretty privileged upbringing, growing up my dad had some pretty well-paying jobs so I didn't want for nothing. We always had a comfortable and warm place to lay our heads, we were always dressed nicely, had delicious food on our table at each meal time, and after school activities etc. I attended a private girls school from Year 5 (Age 10-11) to Year 11 (Age 16). Tennis lessons which lead to state competitions and swimming which lead to early morning squads, school competitions and championship trophies. My daughter has now caught the swimming bug and is currently in the squad swimming group at Age 10! Proud Mum moment!

By the time my teenage years came around my father was engrossed in his work which often involved long hours and trips away. My mum was pretty much in full blown addiction, they were just doing the best they could, with what they could, pretty much what most of you are now doing.

I started to rebel, I did anything I could to get my parents' attention regardless of how good or bad it was. My teenage years were an endless cycle of sneaking out, smoking cigarettes and marijuana, underage drinking, depression, therapy, confusion, boys, isolation and despair, in no particular order.

By 19 I had spent 3 years in and out of school, home, jobs and boyfriends with no clear direction or purpose. It was then that my knight in shining armor came to my no directional life (laugh out loud moment). Haha, we are back to the fairytale! It does happen in the end, keep reading! A tall dark handsome man with a larger than life job as a talented and well known DJ. I latched on and became codependent, all I wanted was love, validation, acceptance for who I was. 7 years later I was divorced, single and still had no direction or identity. How I could have used the guidance of the Lord in my life at this point in time! I spent the next 4-5 years in a whirlwind of drama. I had gone from being Rapunzel locked in a tower, fairytale again, to be as free as a bird. I did do and try everything and anyone I could at the time just to feel wanted, included, accepted and loved. It wasn't too long before I was caught up in what I thought was the glamorous and exciting life of the Melbourne underworld. Money, drugs, Illegal activities, guns, stripping, men that you certainly wouldn't introduce to your mother! Situations that realistically we would never get involved in. But we all know what goes up must come down and I soon realized that if I wanted any kind of normal life or to live, I would have to leave that all behind.

And I did. I moved up to Cairns. My sister had moved up there previously and had 2 young children. I lived with her family for a while but again I got enticed back into the same scene and knew I couldn't continue. I hung around Cairns for a while but as my life went on, I still didn't have any clear direction and I constantly was doing donuts! When my sister and her family moved further up north, very far up north to pursue a different life. I followed a few years after hoping to break the cycle of my pointless life, hoping a switch would turn on and I would finally know what I wanted to do. I surrounded myself with family, it would be great, and it was.

Now this place is as remote as it gets! Generator power, no running water unless you know how to set that all up yourself, cut off from civilization, stranded in the wet season, only access was by boat or 4wd and supplies came in by barge in the wet. A real eye opener for myself, a city girl from Melbourne. I was appointed the Nanny for my nieces, facilitating distance education or attempting to! Camp cook, occasional fishing and general all rounder. It was there of all places I met what I thought would be my second husband, On the banks of the river, in the middle of nowhere, a rough and rugged third generation commercial fisherman with a not so nice reputation. Within a month I was smitten and within 3 months he had put a ring on it. In hindsight, I knew he had done this so I felt obligated to stay, and I did stay. For 12 years, living another man's life once again not my own. For many years, I lived the life of a fisherman's wife although not officially married. Nomadic boat life, 24/7, no days off, no slacking off, always work to be done. He ran a tight ship (boat) and you or things weren't up to his standard you soon knew about it. I brushed off these instances as nothing. He was tired, stressed, busy, and had a lot on his plate. As these "instances" became more frequent, they became more concerning. The extreme reactions, escalating anger, controlling behaviour, but I just let it go. I was "in love", I was wanted, needed and accepted so I endured the uncomfortability for the moments of happiness. And when I look back now, he knew no better, he was brought up with tough love, a hard life, he was definitely a product of his environment. I do not regret a single moment in my life or this relationship because it is in these experiences we grow and learn and determine what we don't want in our lives later on. Yes, life was tough at that time, the environment and lifestyle was gruelling but I had some of the most amazing experiences in my life. I've travelled Australia from one side to the other and its circumference by boat, plane, 4wd, truck and campervan. I've seen so many places of unspeakable beauty, rugged landscapes, vast oceans, endless skies, billions of stars and a multitude of amazing creatures that our heavenly father created, if you believe in him doing that. I will probably never see anything else like that in my life again so I am so thankful for being able to live that life at that time. I've gained qualifications and skills that I never thought I would have.

About 7 years into the relationship I fell pregnant, not really planned, but not actively preventing pregnancy. We were happy, most of the time and 9 months later our boy came into the world. A strapping healthy boy 3.6kgs gently flowed into this world via a surreal and peaceful water birth. Being in and around water has always been my happy place. As the days turned into weeks with my new bundle of joy, my partner had to go back fishing and I was left holding the baby literally. My days were filled with the bliss of new love and the challenges of being a new mum flying by the seat of my pants! Then the unthinkable happened, and from that day my world started to crumble. At 5 weeks old my beautiful boy died. Later on the coroner determined it was SIDS. My days were a blur of sadness, anger, grief, disbelief, confusion, sorrow and guilt. Our families rallied together to comfort each other in terrible circumstances. It was no more than 2 weeks after this that my partner demanded that I go back up to the boats where he could keep his "eye" on me.

My haze continued wherever I was.

Nothing was ever discussed.

The tragic circumstances came and went, the whole instance was brushed under the carpet. And it has never been discussed to this day. I turned to alcohol to numb the pain, the grief, the loss and the days turned into weeks, months with no change. He began to drift away from me, our relationship became distant, business-like, and then like a miracle from God I was pregnant again. I spent the next few months in disbelief and uncertainty, searching for something in a bottle. Not the kind of start you want your child to have but I had no idea how else to cope, I was alone emotionally and mentally, I was now 40 pregnant and still grieving the loss of my son. I was advised by my midwife to relocate closer to support services and medical assistance so they could closely monitor my pregnancy and mental health, so a decision was made to relocate back to Cairns full time. My partner wasn't very agreeing with this but he had no choice but to allow it to happen. I continued to travel back and forth from the boats to cairns, driving fuel and supplies, bringing back bulk fish to sell. As my due date drew near I was spiraling, the regular trips, the huge responsibilities were taking a toll on my health, my mental health was still suffering and my weight was plummeting. I was advised to be prepared to birth early because of all these contributing factors and we found out it was a girl, Thank God. The anxiety I had felt going into this pregnancy was crippling from what had happened to my son, so to say I was relieved was an understatement. She arrived safely, small and 4 weeks early and spent time in the NICU. On one hand, I was extremely blessed that my daughter was physically perfect considering the mental health struggles and my battle with alcohol. On the other hand, I was consumed by guilt, I had not focussed on my pregnancy, my health, well being and therefore my daughters health had suffered. Although my partner seemed happy enough he wasn't as bonded to our daughter as he was to our son. He had completely retreated, we barely spoke unless it was about him, what he wanted or needed for himself or for the business. The next 4 years was a cycle of me, my beautiful girl and my other life. The relationship between my partner and I continued to worsen, it was business like, nothing else, he was demanding, rude, angry, controlling. I realized that in fact what I was going through with him was abuse and although not physical at the time it was every other sort you can think of. Narcissism, gaslighting, control, financial, emotional, mental abuse, withdrawing affection when he didn't get what he wanted, silent treatment. It was exhausting. By the time our daughter was 4 years old, the only time we saw each other was when he "demanded" I drive 700 kms, which took approx. 24 hours due to road conditions and other challenges along the way. Up to the boats to take fuel, stores, supplies whatever they were low on as I rarely went up there and bring back bulk fish to offload to our wholesaler. More often than not it was in the middle of the night in the cloak of darkness due to his paranoia and all this while caring for a small child. The only time she got to be with her dad was after she had spent hours in the truck, cranky from bouncing around, confined to her seat for hours at a time. He barked orders while unloading and loading the truck bossing us all around. Towards the end of the relationship I suppose I just gave up, I was over the drama, it was no way to live and not the type of life I wanted for my daughter growing up. That last year was unbearable. My drinking had increased as I was so unhappy with my life, my grief from losing my son was still there under the surface, being stuck in a relationship with an abusive, controlling, narcissistic man who didn't care about anyone but himself. I was isolating us for fear of this abuse and just wanted to stay in this little bubble of bliss with myself and my daughter. I certainly didn't want to take any more trips up the gulf unless vitally necessary. I didn't want my girl to be exposed to him and his family's disgusting and inexcusable behaviour.

Unfortunately, all the family are tarred with the same brush. And to top it all off, he was unfaithful many times and others were fully aware of this. When I pointed this out or voiced my displeasure I was shut down, your crazy, your being completely ridiculous that not happening at all it's all in your imagination. The final incident that made me realise I had to take a stand and leave this situation behind was when he turned up at our house one afternoon furious, ranting and raving because I had ignored his phone calls, hadn't gone up the boats when I was told and he completely lost it. He physically and verbally abused me in front of our 4 year old daughter. Items were smashed around us while she hung onto me for dear life. She was screaming in my ear,

"NO DADDY, I DON'T WANT TO GO WITH YOU!"

While he tried to drag and pull her off me. When he realised that he didn't have that power over her he stormed off in a huff, got in my truck and drove off through the closed gates never to be seen again. To this day myself or my daughter have not seen him for 7 years, but who's counting! I had certainly had enough this time and I was taking my life back for the sake of myself and my daughter, normally I would have let this go but not anymore. I called the police for the first time in 12 years. They issued an 18mth DVO and after a few weeks we left Cairns and moved south for a new life as far away as we could get. I thought I had done the right thing for my daughter and I, getting moving to a new place, a new life. But I was still mourning the loss of my son and now the loss of my 12 year relationship. I had no job, no money, again no direction, no purpose and still didn't know who I was. I had just spent 12 years living the life of another man. What he wanted, his life, not my own again. What are you doing you silly woman?

We settled in easily enough. My girl started prep and life was going relatively smoothly. I wasn't working but I managed to keep my days busy pottering around the house, making it our home. I was still drinking though not really to excess, well, I thought so anyway. I was managing to function most days, although anxiety was starting to creep its way in through the cracks. We barely went out unless it was to the shops or school. I was terrified he would find us; I was terrified he would take her from me, she was my security blanket and my reason for staying relatively sober. The absences started pretty sporadically at first every now and again, then more frequently I became highly anxious, agoraphobic, depressed, lost and just a mess. Missing school became a common occurrence because I was either lonely, depressed, anxious, hungover, scared or all of the above and it was completely and utterly selfish. Then life just went completely haywire. I lost my license for DUI, after reports to child safety regarding excessive absences and some other concerning reports my daughter was collected from school by relatives. And I was all alone to wallow in my self pity. It was a horrible, depressing time and those 2 years became a bottomless pit of addiction, drama and times I would very much like to forget. My birthday which just happened the day after my daughter was picked up from school, was absolutely the worst day ever. I tried really hard to stay sober for 3 months. My dad came to visit and I knew for his sake I had to keep it together. He has been my constant rock through all of this and I didn't want to let him down. When he left it was a disaster. I went from week to week with no purpose in life, my addiction spiraled from a couple of nights to 4,5,6 days binges. I was often hospitalized because not only was I drinking huge amounts of alcohol for days at a time, I was not eating or drinking water, not taking care of my health at all. I became extremely depressed, I was often psychotically drunk, angry and out of control, yelling, crying and suicidal so was often on a 48hr watch. I was seeing AODS counsellor but I was just telling them what they wanted to hear. My dad however saw the real picture. He called me every single day to check on me. He knew that if I didn't answer I was most likely on one of my binges and if 2 days went by with no contact, he would call the police for a welfare check which usually resulted in an ambulance being called. I was normally heavily intoxicated, belligerent, argumentative, angry and often emotionally distraught. This went on for a period of 12 months approximately, with the episodes becoming more frequent. By March 2022 when my dad arrived to visit to help me celebrate my 50th birthday I was thinking about rehab although not very seriously. There were always barriers to me going, can't afford it, what about my pets, what about my lease? I wasn't ready to commit.

Then it happened. I had a dream. My mum who had passed away a few years prior, came to my house and when I opened the door after a brief conversation she said "Come on we are going to rehab in Hervey Bay!" I contemplated the idea more; I spoke to my AODS counsellor, asked her to find out if there was indeed a rehab in Hervey Bay. Well, there was, she gave me the number. Transformations was called a "peer to peer " therapeutic community. I called both campus's Hervey Bay and the Gold Coast. I researched them online, contemplated my situation and everything just fell into place. I now know that God had sent my mum in the form of one of his angels to give me a message. He was there in the background working out all the finer details which is what I came to understand later. A great close friend who needed a place to live was able to take over my lease, take care of my pets, and keep an eye on my plants, belongings.

From the moment I walked through the gates at Transformations I had a sense of peace wash over me. I knew and still know to this day

I am in the right place. God sent me here as he knew what I needed to overcome my demons and my addiction. My initial plan was to stick it out for 6 months, I'm still here, 1 year later and about to graduate from the program. In the beginning I just had the focus of one hour, one day, one week at a time. Now I cannot believe where the time has gone! I am worthy, I am loved and I am 1 year sober!

I always believed there was a higher power but I was skeptical about the whole 'God' thing. But as I began to see the miracles God was performing here through people recovering from addiction I was and am believing more and more in the power of our Almighty Father. The difference the Transformations program makes not only in our lives but in the lives of everyone around us is amazing. God's power is infinite and unfathomable. In my eyes he surely does exist and although we cannot see him, he is right there by our sides every single day guiding our steps. I am not alone and I don't have to be alone. I now not only have God, I have an amazing group of supporters and friends I have met along the way and together we are fighting the good fight of recovery.

When I first arrived here, I didn't feel worthy of God's love or forgiveness, I didn't believe I was worthy of receiving prayer or praying for something myself. But as time has gone by, I have forgiven myself as I know that the Lord has forgiven me for all I have done. I pray daily and also pray for others.

Psalm 119:105 says: "Your word is a lamp to my feet and a light on my path" With this verse in mind I meditate on his word daily, journalling my thoughts, feelings, giving praise to him and sincerity in my prayers. It's amazing when I reflect on those pages written and how he has answered my prayers or given me a sign that I am on the right path. He is watching 24/7 and he loves every one of us regardless of how bad or good we are.

When we surrender to the Lord and give our heart to serving him, we are born again. "I am a new creation in Christ" 2 Corinthians 5:17

Reflecting on my life up until now, I guess I can say that from my teenage

From years onwards I never really had a reason to love myself.

Self-Love is defined as an appreciation for one's self. How can we develop self-love when the one person who we look up to for guidance has no appreciation for their own self. My mum was caught in a cycle of declining mental health, childhood trauma and debilitating physical injuries that caused her immense pain and suffering. She turned to prescription medication and alcohol to cope with these challenges which through no fault of her own led to addiction. I am not surprised that after enduring all of this my mum had no self-love.

Self-Love motivates us to behave positively.

When we act in a way that supports our physical, psychological and spiritual growth our self-love increases.

We need to have a high regard for our own well-being and happiness. Don't sacrifice your well-being for others.

Self-Love empowers us to take risks and set healthy boundaries for the things that don't work for us. Through doing this we build our own self compassion, take care and responsibility for our own needs and ourselves, lowering our stress and striving for our success. When we do all of this our mental health improves, we will have higher self-esteem, more motivation and healthier relationships.

When we have Self Love it is easier for others to love us and we enjoy the feeling of being loved in return.

Every day the Lord blesses me with his love. I have hope, joy and peace with him, from him, for myself and for others. The presence of his Holy Spirit fills me every day with his power and a purpose that I have never had before in my life.

"For I know the plans I have for you" declare the Lord, "plans to prosper and not to harm you, plans to give you a hope and a future" Jeremiah 29:11

It is only through the Transformations program that I have found my identity through Christ. I am a new creation, a child of God. I am loved, valued, appreciated, validated by the Lord and myself because I know he loves me unconditionally. I have just been accepted to study Chaplaincy and Ministry at University, with the view of becoming a School Chaplain to help our youth navigate modern society and rise to their victory. Pretty good for a woman who never had a plan or purpose!

"I can do all things through Christ who strengthens me" Phillipians 4:13

I have chosen to surrender, to follow God's will, to be led by his light along my yellow brick road all the way to my Princess Palace and my victory! There my knight in shining armor will ride away into the sunset and I will live happily ever after in a world of God's Love.

Oh wait? Oops am I back in my fairytale? Or was that all just a dream?

If you or your loved one need help with addiction please call Transformations Hervey Bay (07) 4194-6621

CHAPTER 20

Learning How To Live, Lead, And Love With Self-Love

Laila Ansari

'The secret in the desire of wanting to do better in life begins with looking inwards. This is where the magic and the true enrichment of your life lives'.

Living below the line

Have you ever felt like giving up?

Not only giving up on your pursuit of something but giving up altogether!

Have you felt like you have tried your hardest to get somewhere with every ounce of your being and still not succeeded?

Resulting in feeling ashamed, useless, unworthy, and ultimately dumb for not preventing the constantly repeated outcome every time.

Alicia Ann Wade

That was me nearly 25 years ago. You see, all I truly ever wanted in life was to be loved and equally love someone in return. Simple!! Well, not in my case. In my reality, it was not easy at all, and many times I ended up thinking, 'Why was this seemingly very small thing, so huge to achieve'. I spent so many years perfecting being what I thought others wanted me to be! I played it safe to ensure I didn't fall out of line or rock the boat in the wrong direction, or so I thought. On the surface, I was an easy-going, intelligent, happy, go-lucky woman. I was funny and fun. A good friend, a dutiful daughter and big sister, a caring, nurturing person, a loyal and dedicated employee, and someone willing to help most strangers without a second thought. So why was I coming home many days and nights feeling loathsome to the core? Unseen, unheard, unloved?

We had only been married for 2 years. He was everything I thought I wanted. Quick-witted, charming, adventurous, caring, self-assured, alluring, a great father to his two young children and determined towards his pursuits in life. We loved each other deeply and intensely. When we were together, the world disappeared, and I felt at home and complete. He was my best friend. In between sharing his two young children with his ex, our weekends were filled with curling up together to watch a movie, spending long hours riding our bikes off road through the forests, having a scrumptious picnic by a stream while we fished or in bed all day enveloped in each other's arms. Life really couldn't get any better. So how did this feeling quickly move away into something more toxic and enmeshed as time went on. How did my happily ever after become my invisible gilded cage. The beauty. The love intoxication. The belonging. How had this become so very short lived and replaced with jealousy, mistrust, suspicion, snide remarks, arguing daily and verbal abuse. My heart was breaking, and I was bewildered as to how I found myself in this situation. In desperation to change my circumstances and regain what I unwittingly lost, I evolved into something I never imagined and had no idea the damaging effects it would have moving forward. I decided to do whatever I needed to ensure I would regain the stability we had in our relationship at the beginning. I was willing to isolate myself from family, friends, work colleagues to immerse myself in changing the outcome of where we ended up.

As the days and weeks moved forward, I was feeling exhausted, frazzled, on edge and very empty. I needed help but as I had withdrawn from almost everyone, I didn't think I could share this with anyone without being judged and taking off the mask that everything was great when it really wasn't. A sudden wash of my past came rushing through me to times where I either wanted to be rescued from my pain or wanted to rescue someone else so I could feel wanted. I acquired or learned this pattern so I could receive a sense of love. However, to receive this love meant pain and sacrifice, and endless amounts of giving myself away, time and time again. Then a small voice inside of me said, 'you have been here before, feeling trapped and unloved.' This new knowing made me sob at my realisation and the helplessness I was feeling in that moment of not knowing; how to get out?

The human spirit is an amazing phenomenon. In all our upbringings, things happen to us which have impacted us and left a long lasting, sometimes negative imprint on our emotions. Sometimes it can be quite unnoticeable and seemingly harmless like emotional or physical neglect. For others, it can be more impacting with sexual abuse or different variations of violence and abuse. Our intuition (otherwise known as our spirit), that part of us that has been inside of us since our existence, does not know how to lie to us! We hear it calling us. Telling us what we need to know about things or someone, but no one teaches you how to connect with it and trust in 'its knowing' for our better good. Nevertheless, when we are all alone, hurting, grieving, regretting and feeling out of control and ultimately yearning for change, one of those voices within us will creep out and say;

You deserve better than this.
You are not a horrible person.
One day you can leave and show them you are not like them.
You are not stupid and worthless.
You will be a better parent when you have a child.
You can do things that are right and good.
Your life is not ruined by your past.
You do not need to continuously make bad choices.
Remember the lessons you have learned from your past.
Trust in yourself.
Do not give up on yourself.
And so many more….
Once you begin to listen to your intuition, what do you do to change where you are?

The catalyst for change

So, why didn't I recognise the hallmarks on the morning I woke up and decided I would attempt to end my life once and for all? Where was that inner fighting spirit protecting me like it had many times before? It had now been 2 more years since I realised my marriage was falling apart and not much had improved or shifted. NO! Instead, just like that, I decided I couldn't take it anymore. I was done. Not another day of manipulation. Guilt. Anger. Accusations of infidelity. Loneliness. Dishonesty and Control.

The constant betrayal of sucking me in, making me feel and believe everything would be okay to gain my trust, only to strip everything away from me again, day after day, after day. I was still hiding the truth from my family and friends. I wasn't going it alone like before. I learned to reach out to a few people around me who offered support and compassion which helped me up until now. That morning I knew I could not suffer another day of being trapped in the name of love. My world turned upside down in an instant and I realised nothing was going to improve or change. Once again things seems to be getting better and we were doing better and getting along. We were seeking marriage counselling, and though it seemed like a long road ahead, I was optimistic we could weather these hard times and still live happily ever after. I was still so desperately in love and obsessed with getting my marriage back on track and feeling 'good' as it did, in the early days. As I walked down the stairs that morning, I just knew where we were heading. Not again. Please. No. I refuse to walk the road we walked repeatedly. As our argument ensued, I remember telling him, 'I will take my own life' if we continued down the same pattern of conversation. The relentless grilling about the night before out with my girlfriends. His response for me was like striking the first match on a gas-lit fire as I was immediately told to go and kill myself off his property. In devastation, I downed a few fistfuls of painkillers and ran out the door for the woods not far from our home. Where was I going to go from here? I had no money because I had relinquished having a bank account and all my earnings went to him. There was no plan B. Death seemed a lesser fate than the shame I was feeling in that moment of deep sadness.

Hours later I was lying in the hospital, not knowing how I got there. As I woke up out of my hospital bed after trying to take my life, I realized I was still alone. Where was my husband? What would happen to me now? I just wanted peace. I was so weary of the battling. I wanted him to know I could be trusted. I wanted him to know there was no one else. There wasn't ever anyone else. I only lived to love, to serve and to adore him. As I looked around at the group of strangers' faces staring at me, I instantly just wanted to be back home and began to cry. A nurse came over to comfort me and asked what she could do to help me? She offered for me to phone my husband so I could be picked up. Until this day, I have no recall of the length of time I spent there. When he arrived, he was distant and cold. My heart sank even deeper.

It wasn't long I returned to the hospital to gain a clean bill of health from the psychiatric department because attempting suicide was a chargeable offense (in the United Kingdom). I had been to see my GP in the past about my mental health. I had been signed off work years before for stress leave also, however no one had ever used the words the Doctor used that day. After a brief conversation with interest into what led me to do what I had done the previous weeks, she turned to me and said, 'Are you aware, you're suffering from verbal abuse? And in some cases verbal abuse is worse than physical because it can go on unnoticed for years because there are no obvious signs of it occurring. It isn't your fault, and would you like us to help you with people who can assist you to get out of the relationship?' My mind was blown. What? Verbal abuse. Me? No way. I took the numbers to reach out too and returned to my marital home. What she said never left my mind, despite my shock and denial of her referencing my life. Ironically, that moment was enough along with the support and love of my family to pivot my thinking and create a ripple effect of small steps in a different direction.

The awakening

'Sooner or later, we must all accept the fact that in a relationship, the only person you are dealing with is yourself. Your partner does nothing more than reveal your stuff to you. Your fear! Your anger! Your pattern! Your craziness! As long as you insist on pointing the finger out there, at them, you will continue to miss out on the divine opportunity to clear your stuff. Here is a meantime tip – We love in others what we love in ourselves. We despise in others what we cannot see in ourselves.' Inyanla Vanzant, In the Meantime: Finding Yourself and the Love You Want

I knew that I no longer wanted to feel the pain I was feeling on an ongoing basis. I knew there was more to my life undiscovered. I knew I needed to move forward in a different direction but gees, no one said how even harder that part was going to be! I had no idea what lay ahead in my future and I was still so overly in love with a man I knew I had no future. I reached out to a friend who physically came and helped me pack all my belongings which forced me to leave. From that moment on, I had committed to myself I was going to create a different outcome for myself than the one I had accepted as my status quo. The terminology of "self-love was very alien to me. I had no idea how to demonstrate it, provide examples of it, and understand how to achieve it. So, I asked myself, "How do I begin to practise self-love?" What are the steps that I can take to create a new me?

I read my first self-help book called, "In the Meantime". I felt so inspired and connected with the words that were written on the page about how the author had overcome mental and physical abuse, abusive relationships, homelessness, and just being completely and utterly unloved by herself and by those around her. That was the beginning of the turning point in my life where I really understood what it was like to live in the basement of my mind. To say that you want good things to happen to you. Yet, creating and thinking and being the opposite of what you say you want, and want to welcome into your life. To shed all those negative thoughts, feelings, actions, and energy I really needed to go back to the base of recognising if I wanted my life and my life circumstances to change, then I was the one who needed to change. I needed to stop blaming those around me for the things that had happened out of my control and take ownership and responsibility for how I could live starting today. I was always a happy child. I loved people. I loved nature. I loved the feeling of putting a smile on other people's faces and being acknowledged however, somewhere along my journey, I lost my way and, in the process, lost control of who I was. This book was the medicine my subconscious soul needed to re-ignite my internal light. Needless to say, I was not even sure what self-love meant beyond presenting myself well to the world, which for me was still wearing a mask to portray a role I did not truly embody. What self-love meant and how to be consistent with my demonstration of it was something I took years to truly understand and live by. Somewhere along my voyage back to self, I was encouraged to write some affirmations down on paper and place them somewhere I would see them every day with the intention to read them daily. The caveat was I also needed to read them in front of a mirror and look at myself as I read. Little did I know, carrying out this task was a very powerful tool for reconnecting with myself and looking deeply into my pained heart and allowing myself the ability to heal and love myself for all I never recognised me for.

My affirmations went something like this:

1. I am worthy of love. Capable of giving and receiving love.
2. I am beautiful. I embrace and celebrate my uniqueness.
3. I am a good person with good intentions.
4. Good things will happen to me if I believe they will.
5. I am deserving of success and happiness.
6. I forgive myself for the mistakes I have made.
7. I forgive others for the pain they have caused me.
8. I am enough just the way I am.
9. I have the power to choose my future and where I go.
10. I am light. I am love and I am joy.

I would wake up every day and recite my words of affirmation to myself. To start off with, it was not an easy task. There was a lot of resistance and physical objection to staring at myself in the mirror. Because I didn't believe any of the words I was saying, my body was rejecting the notion to recite it. Despite my feelings, I did the work more mornings than not and some days were easier while some days didn't happen at all. Without my conscious awareness, I was cultivating a stronger sense of self love within me for which the benefits are still withstanding until today. The affirmations helped me harness the following:

1. **Shifting negative self-talk** that had gone rampant inside my mind daily. I began the process of stopping myself before I began spiralling into a dark space so my turn around became shorter and shorter until having the negative self-talk was nearly eliminated with time.
2. **Boosting self-confidence** by helping me recognise through my reading and affirmations, helped me reinforce a more positive image of myself and in my ability to change my future self. Regularly affirming my worth, strengthened my ability to believe I could reach for higher goals and dreams of accomplishment.
3. **Strengthening my self-identity** by creating a more positive perception of myself. I never felt pretty or worthy however when reciting my daily affirmations, I began to develop a healthier relationship with myself and have a clearer understanding of what I valued.
4. **Cultivating self-acceptance** was fundamental to my healthy mindset. I needed to see and feel the value of my uniqueness and stop wishing to be anything other than myself. I started to feel more authentically me instead of being what I thought others wanted me to be.

5. **Improving my self-compassion** with acknowledging I will make mistakes as I have in the past and this doesn't remove me from being a good, well intended person. My focus moved away from my imperfections and towards building upon my stronger attributes.
6. **Enhancing my emotional well-being and mindset** when I consistently repeated my affirmations, my body started to act out on the meanings I was giving it. The reinforcement in my mind made me more focused on creating bigger and better goals for myself and being more emotionally resilient.

In the end it took a couple of years looking in the mirror to really like what I saw and feeling at peace with who I was. That feeling I needed to show up for anything or anyone other than myself was gone. I now believed the words of love. The words of worthiness and empowerment. I continued to recite my affirmations until one day I woke up not needing to read the words as I could hear my mind reciting the words already as I got ready. The affirmations were my catalyst for showing up every day with consistency. Leaving me feeling ready and alive to face my days ahead.

Once I learned the way back to myself, which meant being able to look at myself in the mirror and look deeper than my skin's surface. I needed to see the person beneath the makeup. Underneath the nice clothes, and possibly often, the false smile. I needed to fully embrace and love 'ME' with all her faults, flaws, imperfections, limitations, fears, regrets, sorrows, dreams and desires. And wholeheartedly knowing I was okay and would continue to be okay with my newfound understanding of my relationship with myself. When I knew I would allow myself to fall in love again with clearer understanding on loving me would always come first and foremost. Meaning I would never forsake my own self-love to demonstrate love for someone else. When I had this self-awareness, self-love began to show up and pronounce itself to me in ways I never thought I would experience, feel, or be able to express. Learning how to live, lead, and love with self-love first has given me back to myself. I am the master of my ship. If my crew decides to commit mutiny, I know I still have control over my destiny and how I decide to navigate the waters of life!

Since 2019, I have been working as an Empowerment Coach for professional women looking to find deeper love within themselves so they can share this with someone else. Looking back over the past 20+ years on my journey towards myself has led me to identify the need to share my story to inspire, encourage and provide some tiny steps to believing in a different future for yourself or someone else. If some of my story resonates with you and you would like my complimentary gift called, *'Creating Smooth Communication Skills'* with the purchase of this book, please reach out to me on social media under, Laila Ansari for Facebook or @Laila.Ansari. Coaching on Instagram.

My website is also www.lailaansari.com

My leaving thoughts for you are a famous quote from Frank Zappa someone told me during my troubled state. The quote says,

'A mind is like a parachute. It works better when it's open.'

CHAPTER 21

Acceptance Of Oneself Is Self-Love

Hazel Vertley

"Self-acceptance and self-discovery are ongoing processes that I now define as self-love. Understanding my own needs, wants, and desires and then acting to fulfil them is key. Additionally, it involves accepting my own shortcomings and mistakes while also being kind and compassionate to myself and learning from them."

For me, self-love results from a variety of relationships and life experiences. The more I mature, the more I understand that we all have demons and that each person's approach to overcoming them will be unique.

An individual's perception of and love for themselves are significantly influenced by society. An individual's perception of themselves and their value as a person is influenced by society in the ways listed below:

Social norms and expectations: People are frequently assessed on how well they conform to society's standards for success, behaviour, and appearance. The result may be low self-esteem and feelings of inadequacy.

Media representation: Narrow beauty standards and gender roles are frequently reinforced by the media, especially advertising and popular culture, which makes people feel under pressure to fit in.

Comparison with others: The temptation to compare oneself to others can be heightened by social media and other forms of communication, which can result in feelings of insecurity and a distorted perception of one's own value.

Family and friends: The views and behaviours of those closest to us, such as family and friends, can have a significant impact on how we perceive ourselves and how valuable we are.

I was surrounded by a lot of love as I was growing up. My mother, my little brother, my grandparents, and my uncles were my roommates. I never had any doubts about my grandmother's love for me because she embodied everything you would expect a mother to be: loving, caring, and gentle in her own way. For me, my uncle Tino was like a father; he picked me up from school, accompanied me as he commuted to work, and attended my school's musical performances. He served as the father figure in my life, and having these two incredible people in my life makes me feel beyond blessed.

When I was 3 years old, my father abandoned my mother. Do I recall? No, but I do recall the subsequent events that led to self-doubt and resentment towards my mother in me as a young child. My father was absent from my life. My recollection of him as a child is that he would say he was coming, but he was very absent. We would get excited and wait, but he never showed up and never even called. I also remember clearly when I was a young child—maybe 6 years old—my mother telling me that my dad was coming home for Christmas and going out to buy him presents for the tree, and guess what? He never returned. It was at that point that we learned he was married and expecting a child. These things caused me to question who I was as a child. I used to question my father, "Does he love me?" or "What have I done wrong that he doesn't want to see me and my brother?" As a young girl, I was unaware of the impact this would have on me as I grew up.

I had a lot of self-consciousness about how I looked and how I appeared as a teenager. I used to be a chubby teen and child. People would always comment on how dark I was as a child or refer to me as black Chinese because I am half Asian or Italian. I was ethnic with dark skin and dark features. As a child, I recall wishing that I were lighter and that my hair was lighter, but I later came to appreciate the beauty of my skin and hair, learned that people go to the beach to tan in order to have my skin tone, and discovered that I was naturally dark and didn't need to do anything to change that.

Years of Rebellion: I began using drugs when I was 15 years old. My close friend and I started using heroin. My dad's absence really hurt and affected me as a child, which I suppose contributed to my confusion about life. At the age of 15, I briefly ran away from home. In addition to smoking a lot of heroin at the time, I also got a tattoo. It was similar to when I was high because I wasn't bothered by anything and was given a lot of the attention I craved from those around me. I began using Ecstasy at the age of 16, and it completely changed my life. I didn't smoke heroin anymore. I began using ecstasy on the weekends. I would experience such euphoria and self-love in that situation. By the time I was 18, I switched from weekends to weekdays, and I was legally taking 10 to 20 pills every weekend to get completely off my face. Looking back, I can see that this was how I dealt with my anxieties, negative thoughts, and insecurities in life.

18-24 total I don't remember much, to be honest. You name it, I did it: I was snorting coke, smoking ice, and popping Ecstasy. Drugs evolved into a way to escape reality. There was always a bad comedown. My anxiety would skyrocket whenever I got into my head. Being straight was the worst. In my head, it seemed as though all of my demons were awake and engaged. I would experience mental games in my head.

I once had a drug-fueled obsession with my appearance, a good body, people liking me, and guys liking me. During these times, I also began to experience severe anxiety. The drugs didn't help; I would still experience panic attacks and mental confusion. I'm relieved I made it through these six years, which seemed like a lifetime and hurt my physical, mental, and emotional well-being.

When I became pregnant at age 24, it saved my life because I was able to stop using drugs, smoking, and even working throughout my pregnancy. I was so anxious and wanted to make sure that nothing went wrong. Nine months later, I gave birth to my daughter, who has since become my greatest success and the love of my life. I have never loved anyone with the same intensity as I do my child, and I was so preoccupied with being a mother that I worried constantly about my daughter.

Even just by writing down the events and things that happened in my life in this point-by-point format, I can now see how traumatic some of those events were for me and am better able to understand who I am and how my mind works. Each person has their demons, but mine are much worse. What you might think is insignificant to someone else may not be.

Even as an adult, I still feel hurt, but I've learned to put things in perspective. I've grown to love myself enough to realise that I'm valuable regardless of how I look or what society deems attractive. From within, beauty emanates. Kindness is what makes a person beautiful; it is not something that can be seen on the outside of a person. The people who made me feel insecure, who felt like they needed to put something down to feel better, were the ones who called me fat, black, or said I had dirty skin. Now I see that.

If you know me, you will be able to tell when I am hurt, sad, or happy because I tend to hide my demons behind humour and my ability to be a joker. I tend to give more to people whose attention I still crave because I am by nature a giver. I now advocate for treating others with kindness, love, and compliments. Being a good person and buying a stranger a coffee because, at 43, I finally love myself, and my body, and want to continue to develop and love every aspect of myself. To help you understand me and perhaps relate to it, I've provided a timeline of my life in point form.

I now prefer to surround myself with uplifting, like-minded individuals and maintain a small circle of friends, but those who are in my circle are people I genuinely love and who are all aware of who they are. I want to keep developing as a person. I want to understand myself and my emotions better. I always have been and always will be a giver who loves deeply. That's something I can't change, but I cherish it.

Now that I'm an adult, this is how I define self-love.

Self-acceptance and self-discovery are ongoing processes that I now define as self-love. It involves recognising my own needs, wants, and desires and taking the appropriate action to satisfy them. Additionally, it involves accepting my own shortcomings and mistakes while also being kind and compassionate to myself and learning from them.

Setting and upholding boundaries is another aspect of practising self-love. It's about realising the value of my time, effort, and resources and how they should be invested in accordance with my values and objectives. Saying no to things that don't serve me and taking care of my physical and mental health are part of this.

It also entails looking after my physical health through a healthy diet, consistent exercise, adequate rest, and good hygiene. This enables me to have the vigour and concentration required to handle my daily responsibilities.

Create a journal of gratitude. Every day, list three things for which you are grateful. This will assist you in turning your attention to the good things in your life and enhance your general outlook.

Invest in your well-being by scheduling time for relaxing pursuits like reading, meditation, and exercise. Put self-care first and incorporate it into your daily routine.

Stop self-critical speech: Recognise when you are being self-critical and change the way you are thinking. Try saying, "I made a mistake, but that doesn't define me," rather than, "I'm so stupid."

Spend time with people who uplift you and make you feel good about yourself. Surround yourself with positive people. Keep away from those who are negative.

Set realistic goals: Set attainable objectives and acknowledge small victories along the way. This will promote self-assurance and respect.

Get better at forgiving yourself. We must develop the ability to forgive ourselves for our mistakes because everyone makes them. Moving forwards and loving ourselves can be hampered by holding onto the past.

Utilise mindfulness techniques: Mindfulness is the practice of being in the present moment.

CHAPTER 22

Living with Body Dysmorphic Disorder and learning to love oneself

"Remember we are all imperfectly perfect"

Just a few of the topics I will be covering in my chapter include drug and alcohol abuse, rape and sexual abuse, domestic violence, escorting and fibromyalgia. Although my story is not for the faint of heart, many people in today's society will be able to relate to it or have gone through something similar.

I'm 41 years old and come from parents who's marriage ended when I was 5. My father had an affair so me and my two older siblings lived with our mother rarely visiting our dad.

This did not faze me as he was always very negative and extremely judgmental towards us. Constant remarks about my appearance and how never to become fat or get (rain damage) which is another way of saying cellulite as I would never find someone to love me.

Complaining about the way I would have my hair and what clothes I chose to put on, i was never enough for him. I remember him grabbing my non existent fat when i was around 12 and saying in front of all of his mates 'What's this"? I was actually a thin kid, little did he realize how impacting his comments could be. My dad owned a restaurant and we would go there about twice a year and he would give us leftover food from other peoples platters, this validating his shame towards me. He was ashamed. Embarrassed. He never told us he loved us nor showed any love. Just screamed and judged everything. He made me feel completely rejected that as a child I was asking my mums new boyfriend if he could please be my dad. Funnily enough my mum stayed with this wonderful man to whom I refer to as my dad to this day.

This behavior from my father was the beginning of my low self worth and Body dysmorphic disorder. If my father cant love me and acted ashamed of me then how do I love myself. There's obviously something wrong with me, I developed this mentality at such a young age and at the age of 14 I was diagnosed with BBD by two psychologists.

I was then raped at the age of 14 and was sexually abused several times over the next few years by older school boys and leaving school just attracted abusive, toxic men following more sexual abuse and violations.

I had a rhinoplasty at 15 which came about after continual begging to my mother. She tried to talk me out of it saying I didn't need it but finally caved and took me to a surgeon of which was a family friend. I was somewhat happy with the result but that didn't last long, I would just go on to the next body part or still complain about my nose.

So I was using drugs and alcohol too to deal with my low self-esteem, trying to fit in at school and be cool. I couldn't concentrate at school as I was completely consumed with my appearance, anxiety and depression. This effected my studies, friendships and my quality of life. Now I had no one to talk to about this as I was ashamed and didn't want to look vain as I am not a vain person. BDD is very real and it doesn't discriminate. It has a very high suicide rate. Surveys of people with BDD attending a specialist clinic show about 25% have attempted suicide in the past. What about the people who don't see specialists, and that's a lot because we don't want to draw attention to our body and pin point what we don't like about it, we feel ashamed. Not many people had heard of BDD back when I was diagnosed whereas now its got a lot more publicity. I tried to take my life twice by overdosing on alcohol and xanax but just woke up in hospital with that same nauseous feeling of FUCK I have still have to live as ME.

I tried to focus on the fact that I was a genuinely good person, had a big heart, I was kind and empathetic to everyone. However all I did all day was want to change how I looked. Id get home and stare in the mirror for hours, I would be constantly needing validation from my friends, would cover my face with my long hair in class, I felt self conscious around everyone including my mother. Constantly thinking people were making fun of me and so paranoid whenever anyone toughed their face I was convinced they were mirroring my perceived flaws. I isolated myself and felt like a prisoner in my own body. I've been on countless anti depressants, and seen loads of psychologists …but I just couldn't stop obsessing.

Self-Love

I used to wake up and vomit due to the emotional attachment to this condition, dreading going to school or leaving the house because I didn't want people to look at me. It got so bad that I decided the only way out of this nightmare called reality was more plastic surgery but how? Plastic surgery is expensive. I had finished high school and was using more drugs and alcohol as my coping mechanism and around the age of 22 I decided to sell my body (ironic in hindsight) I called some escorting agencies and booked an interview. This was the by far the scariest day of my life and I've been through some shit so I was absolutely petrified. Shaking scared. This went against all of my morals and beliefs so the desperation to change my appearance was strong enough for me to do something that was completely out of character and I swore I would take to the grave.

Funnily enough I am sharing this story with you, BDD should be taken very seriously, it is not vanity, I cant stress this enough. I know there might be people judging me because they don't understand but for anyone reading this who has BDD or can relate to what I'm saying I just want to tell you I UNDERSTAND. For those of you who don't know anything about Body Dysmorphic Disorder it is a mental illness involving obsessive focus on a perceived flaw. The flaw may me minor or imagined, but the person may spend hours trying to fix it. The person may try many cosmetic procedures or exercise to excess. People with this disorder may frequently examine their appearance in a mirror, constantly compare their appearance with that of others and avoid social situations or photos. It does require a medical diagnosis.

Now back to escorting, I was very fortunate in the clients the agency gave me as I can honestly say I was treated better by them than the men I chose for myself. Such as Domestic violence, being spat on, called every name under the sun. I was bashed once knocked unconscious and locked in a sunroom because I tried to leave him. I just kept attracting the same kind of man treating me like shit because I was a walk over. They would say sorry and I would forgive them. There are only so many excuses you can make up such as I walked into the door, I tripped over the dog ect ect to cover up this visible abuse on my face. This was all relative of my low self worth. I mean I didn't have the best introduction to men starting with my father then losing my virginity by rape, violence and so on and so forth. However using drugs and alcohol was the only way I could do this job. I had to be drunk so I could hopefully forget in the morning as I was ashamed. I was brought up by a very respectable, morally abiding mother and wonderful step father, I went to a good school and was raised in good neighborhoods.

However I was able to get my rhinoplasty again, liposuction twice, cheeks, lower blepharoplasty, genioplasty, Botox and fillers. I just went from one body part to the next never satisfied. I even got an infection in my cheek from a procedure and my face blew up so badly that I could not see out of my eyes. I looked like something from a horror movie. I had to be rushed to hospital to try and drain the infection out of my face before it potentially got into my blood stream. I remember praying and I am not a religious person although raised catholic, I said to god I will never have another procedure just let me be okay. Well that didn't eventuate did it, nope as soon as I was better I was thinking about another operation. This is until I had a bigger wake up call. I found a surgeon in Argentina in Buenos Aires, yep I was seeking surgery now out of Australia. I had to have a translator who helped me get organized for meeting the surgeon in person. She came into the consultation with me and she was very well accustomed to plastic surgery herself as she was actually born a male so she was a transgender and had had gender –affirming surgery which in her case was everything. So during my consultation my surgeon could not really understand what I wanted to achieve. He even suggested that I might have BDD and that he thought I was beautiful and couldn't really see why I was there. I was not satisfied with this at all, I had just flown 23 hours on a plane for surgery, so I was adamant that I was getting surgery. I insisted and he agreed to operate. The night before theatre I got a personal phone call from the surgeon and he was still suggesting that I change my mind. Even saying that he would take me out on a date and show me around Buenos Aires. I could of have had 10 red flags and I still would of done it. So I arrived at the hospital and my room was immaculate, I had already come to the hospital prior just to check it out and it was clean and modern which put my mind at some ease. Although I still couldn't shake this gut feeling that something bad was going to happen, I remember pacing the room back and forth my anxiety was through the roof. So I was taken into theatre and I remember waking up after surgery and there was music playing and I started singing along when I all of a sudden couldn't breath, I was coughing and gasping for air, I could feel my mouth filling up with blood, and I honestly thought this was how I was going to die. The whole room was in panic mode screaming at each other in Spanish, I knew it wasn't good. I got rushed into ICU and had chest xrays showing my lungs filled with fluid. They put tubes down my throat and my surgeon and my anesthetist stayed at the end of my bed the entire night to make sure that I was okay and that I didn't die. Once I flew back to Australia I found out from another plastic surgeon that I had two titanium screws in my chin which baffled him. They were stopping the blood flow to my chin bone which can result in death of bone tissue and the bone can eventually break down and collapse. He had no idea why I had the screws in the first place? I obviously had to get them removed. This was a massive wake up call. So not only did I waste a lot of money on flights, accommodation and surgery, I didn't look any different, had to have corrective surgery to get the screws out and I nearly died in a foreign country.

I ceased escorting after this horrifying experience and decided that I needed to try and love myself just the way Iam otherwise this will never stop. So I got regular jobs and started my own cleaning business entailing of windows, vacates and commercial and domestic contracts and built this up to a nice little business but I still had drug and alcohol issues just to be able to live life and even function. I also had been diagnosed with fibromyalgia around 22 years old a which is a chronic pain disorder. This only effects me when I am trying to sleep which has doctors very confused so my pain being psycho somatic is the general consensus from multiple professionals. Suppressed trauma manifesting itself though my subconscious when I'm sleeping. As soon as I get up this burning aching throbbing terrible pain in my limbs stops. Ive tried everything from neurologists, rheumatologists, neurolinguistic programming, naturopaths, MRIs, CT scans, X-rays, 10 day silent meditation (vipassnana), TFT, hypnosis, acupuncture, 10 day fasting retreats in Bali, not to mention the countless prescribed drugs from my GP's and specialists such as antidepressants, antipsychotics, sedative hypnotics, opiates and benzodiazepines. Now ive rightfully questioned several doctors

Self-Love

motivations for prescribing me certain medications, was it to help me or to help them??. I've now had this horrible condition for nearly 20 years and still have horrible sleep which doesn't help as we all know how important sleep is to your mental heath and our day to day functioning as well.

Then an old friend came back into my life and we ended up living together and we started a relationship based on drugs and our similar issues of severe anxiety and the need for substance to cope on a day to day basis. We ended up falling in love but that soon went toxic as most drug orientated relationships do. We were using ice and GHB continuously, our love for GHB was strong, we were in love with it. It helped set us free of feeling like prisoners in our skin. He had a debilitating anxiety disorder aswel but GHB took that away. We thought we had found our miracle drug. It took away inhibitions, gave confidence, increased libido, made life enjoyable and because id never experienced enjoying life due to my BDD this became problematic real quick. I WAS HOOKED. Id always had drug and alcohol issues but id never loved a drug as much as I loved GHB. I ended up in rehab due to an intervention from my mum and step father. This relationship became extremely unhealthy, violent and abusive. Then we fell pregnant for the second time as I had already miscarried once with him.

So I was 36 now and still suffering with BDD even though I've stopped getting procedures doesn't mean my BDD brain has stopped. It's a daily battle. We would fight about it all the time. So finding out I was pregnant was super exciting as I had now lost 3 pregnancies throughout my life 2 with a previous partner 1 being aborted and the other being a girl she had a omphalocele (a birth defect of the abdominal wall) so I had to terminate at 4.5 months. I was devastated. So being pregnant for the fourth time I though this is what I need to change my life as I had always wanted to be a mother. I quit everything and stayed clean throughout my pregnancy. My partner still drank alcohol but I was happier with that than ice and GHB. After my beautiful daughter Ava was born my relationship went backwards with my partner and I left due to more domestic violence because now I had somebody else I had to protect so I went straight to the police after he attacked me while I was holding her and I dropped her on the ground. Thankfully I was sitting on carpet and low to the floor and she was not hurt. I placed an intervention order on him that day and have never looked back. Even if I cannot love myself, I am determined to be the best mum and role model for her. I don't want her growing up with the same issues as me so I need to love myself to set a good healthy example for my daughter.

Especially in the world we live now with social media such as Twitter, Instagram, TicTok just to mention a few and all the unhealthy body images young girls and boys are exposed to. With an estimated 3.6 billion users world wide social media is a large part of todays culture. Social media can negatively effect body image by over-exposing you to an "idealized" body types. While posting selfies may help body image, trying to edit out perceived flaws can be harmful. It is so important for us to not compare ourselves with others, we are all unique and beautiful in our own individual way. To reduce harm on social media unfollow accounts, find a healthy community and take breaks.

Self-Love

So my daughter is 5 and a half years old now and has started primary school this year, I'm raising her as a single mum and her father has nothing to do with her since I left him when she was three months old. I've decided that id prefer to stay single and just focus on Ava for now as the bar is set a lot higher than what it was for whom I would let in my life to say the least. They would have to treat us with love and respect and know our worth, they would have to be an amazing role model for Ava or im not interested. I am just not settling for anything less.

What we teach our children is huge, the type of role model we are, how we speak about ourselves and others. I never body shame myself in front of my daughter and I never speak disrespectfully or verbalize any judgment on another person's appearance. In fact I look for the beauty in everyone. Our perception of the world can be detrimental to their mental health and self identity. Our perception of the world helps shape their perception of the world. Make it a positive one.

Since I left Ava's father and stayed clean I have finished cert 3 in animal studies, have become a qualified chef, and im in the process of setting up my own catering company. This is coming from somebody who could never finish anything. I finished year 12 but I really should of failed due to lack of attendance due to my mental health. My circle of friends has completely changed and I spend a lot of time involved in my daughters schooling and her outside activities. BDD is still a daily challenge but with Ava as my motivation I will never give up. Ava is teaching me about love everyday and is my saving grace. Before my mum passed away 4 and a half years ago she said "AVA IS YOUR SAVIOUR" and I just love that….

So I still drink alcohol I'm not claiming I'm perfect but its now balanced. My life is drama free and I wouldn't have it any other way. I practice self-love with positive affirmations, mirror work which is by far the hardest and getting out into nature for walks which for me which is very healing. I practice self hypnosis, meditation and daily gratitude, I drink lots of celery juice and eat lots of healthy foods and herbal teas which nourishes my soul, body and mind. Don't get me wrong I still like my junk food too.

All I can say is that we need to build each other up instead of tearing one another down. The more you judge others the more you judge yourself. By constantly seeing the bad in others we train our minds to find the bad in ourselves leading to stress, low self worth, insecurities and isolation. When you stop living your life based on what others think of you, real life begins. At that moment, you will finally see the door of self-acceptance opened. Being happy doesn't mean that everything is perfect, it means that you've decided to look beyond those imperfection. Remember we are all perfectly imperfect.

You are all worthy and totally loveable.

Love, peace and acceptance to you all XXX

Natty

www.ingramcontent.com/pod-product-compliance
Lightning Source LLC
Chambersburg PA
CBHW071953070526
44583CB00015B/1172